P9-BHZ-392
LEVEL 2

MORE
Reading
Comprehension
in Varied Subject Matter

SOCIAL STUDIES

LITERATURE AND LANGUAGE

COMBINED SUBJECTS

PHILOSOPHY, LOGIC, AND MATH

SCIENCE THE ARTS

JANE ERVIN

Educators Publishing Service
Cambridge and Toronto

TO THE STUDENT

Each selection in this workbook is on a theme that reappears in each book in the series. For example, Selection 5 in each book is about "Great Americans"; Selection 12 is about "World of Water, Sea, and Fish," while Selection 25 is on "Personalities in the Arts."

There are also themes and topics within each book. These relate the selections to one another, show different aspects of a topic, and help you to gain a broader knowledge of a subject.

The topics in this book are mysteries and ghosts, how humans treat each other, struggle for survival, and persecution and discrimination. Look for these topics, and how they are treated, as you read the selections.

Educators Publishing Service
800.225.5750
www.epsbooks.com

1999 REVISED EDITION OF READING COMPREHENSION BOOK 8

Copyright © 1999, 1997, 1996, 1993, 1980, 1973, by Educators Publishing Service, a division of Delta Education, LLC. All rights reserved. No part of this book may be reproduced or utilized in any form or by any electronic or mechanical means, including photocopying, without permission in writing from the publisher.

Printed in U.S.A.
ISBN 0-8388-0607-4

18 19 20 PPG 20 19

MORE Reading Comprehension

Revised for 1999 Edition

IN VARIED SUBJECT MATTER
by JANE ERVIN

LEVEL 2

Teacher's Key

SELECTION 2—CONVERSATIONS WITH A GORILLA

THINKING IT OVER
(1) She was taught sign language.
(2) 375.
(3) Not only could she correctly name many things, but, like humans, she could actually use language to express thoughts and feelings.

STUDYING THE PASSAGE
(1) c (2) (a) T (e) T (3) (a) 6 (e) 8 (4) b (5) b
         (b) T (f) F   (b) 7 (f) 1
         (c) F (g) T   (c) 3 (g) 5
         (d) T (h) F   (d) 2 (h) 4

USING THE WORDS
(1) (a) relish   (e) proficiency
    (b) pique   (f) perception
    (c) distort   (g) diverse
    (d) tantalizing (h) empathy

SELECTION 3—THE ONLY WAY TO TRAVEL

THINKING IT OVER
(1) *Any four:* Attach themselves to a larger fish or to the bottom of a ship; cling to feathers of birds; ride on ships; ride on beetles and larger insects; ride on backs of pelicans and turtles.
(2) Wind; insects; clinging spines or hooks; gummy substances, which help seeds stick to passing animals, birds, and humans.

STUDYING THE PASSAGE
(1) d (2) (a) T (e) F (3) (a) 5 (e) 6 (4) c (5) b, c
         (b) T (f) F   (b) 2 (f) 7
         (c) T (g) T   (c) 8 (g) 1
         (d) F (h) F   (d) 3 (h) 4

USING THE WORDS
(1) (a) aquatic   (e) migrant
    (b) mode   (f) aloft
    (c) excursions   (g) ballast
    (d) cross-   (h) evolution
        pollination

SELECTION 4—WILLIAMSBURG, VIRGINIA

THINKING IT OVER
(1) He meant that George III was in as much danger of overthrow as Caesar and Charles were before their downfalls.
(2) Williamsburg today is a museum showing how colonial Americans lived, but the city in Revolutionary times was an important political center, the home of ideas that profoundly affected American history.

STUDYING THE PASSAGE
(1) b (2) (a) F (e) T (3) (a) 2 (e) 5 (4) c (5) a
         (b) F (f) F   (b) 7 (f) 8
         (c) T (g) T   (c) 1 (g) 4
         (d) T (h) F   (d) 3 (h) 6

USING THE WORDS
(1) (a) cobblestone   (f) quartered
    (b) militia   (g) dwindled
    (c) implication   (h) dissent
    (d) treason   (i) radical
    (e) revolution   (j) pervades

SELECTION 5—JOHN F. KENNEDY'S INAUGURAL ADDRESS

THINKING IT OVER
(1) Americans should do something for their country. More specifically, they should commit themselves to the protection of human rights; the defense of freedom; the struggle against tyranny, poverty, disease, and war itself.
(2) The Torch of Freedom. This image recalls the Statue of Liberty as well as the relay of runners (Kennedy's successive generations) carrying the torch from Greece to the site of modern Olympics. It also stands for the responsiblity of new bearers (citizens) to fight for American ideals.
(3) The Call to Battle, with military and Biblical associations. Kennedy means that Americans are still called to struggle for what they believe in.
(4) He wants the listener to become personally involved. The phrases help listeners to identify with the president, and by using them, he shows that he regards himself as an ordinary citizen.

STUDYING THE PASSAGE
(1) a (2) (a) T (e) T (3) (a) 3 (e) 8 (4) c (5) b
         (b) F (f) T   (b) 4 (f) 5
         (c) F (g) T   (c) 7 (g) 6
         (d) T (h) F   (d) 1 (h) 2

USING THE WORDS
(1) (a) summoned   (f) committed
    (b) endeavor   (g) tempered
    (c) testimony   (h) tyranny
    (d) disciplined (i) tempered
    (e) burden

SELECTION 6—JO'S SACRIFICE

THINKING IT OVER
(1) Many answers are acceptable. Most people would still praise Jo because she made a sacrifice for her family. However, many people today would not make such a fuss about the hair itself. Jo would not stand out as odd because now short hair and unusual styles are much more common. They would disapprove of statements such as "Short hair is boyish" and "Oh, Jo, how could you—your one vanity."
(2) It shows the depth of her devotion to him.

STUDYING THE PASSAGE
(1) d (2) (a) T (e) F (3) (a) 5 (e) 7 (4) b, c, d (5) a, c, d
         (b) F (f) T   (b) 6 (f) 3
         (c) T (g) T   (c) 1 (g) 4
         (d) T (h) T   (d) 2 (h) 8

USING THE WORDS
(1) (a) condemned   (f) vanity
     (b) air   (g) assumed
     (c) predicament   (h) rash
     (d) oblige   (i) cropped
     (e). indifferent   (j) awe

SELECTION 7—AN INCREDIBLE RECORD
THINKING IT OVER
(1) Begins in the present, then flashes back, and ends with a look into the future. Also, the passage is organized in terms of the various individuals who affected Mark's life at different times.
(2) *Any three:* Rivalry and ill-feeling from other athletes; keeping to a heavy practice schedule; learning to get along with others; avoiding overconfidence; overcoming nervousness; handling pressure; learning to accept defeat without losing heart.

STUDYING THE PASSAGE
(1) c   (2) (a) T   (e) F   (3) (a) 5   (e) 7   (4) c   (5) b
           (b) F   (f) T   (b) 2   (f) 4
           (c) F   (g) T   (c) 8   (g) 6
           (d) T   (h) F   (d) 1   (h) 3

USING THE WORDS
(1) (a) disdain   (f) touted
     (b) rites   (g) dismal
     (c) perspective   (h) perspective
     (d) brashness   (i) even keel
     (e) mentor   (j) prowess

SELECTION 8—JOAN OF ARC
THINKING IT OVER
(1) The French were desperate.
(2) *Any two:* She broke the siege of Orleans; won many important battles; made it possible for Charles VII to be crowned king; raised the spirits of the French people.
(3) She was burned at the stake.

STUDYING THE PASSAGE
(1) b   (2) (a) T   (e) T   (3) (a) 8   (e) 3   (4) a   (5) d
           (b) T   (f) T   (b) 2   (f) 4
           (c) F   (g) F   (c) 1   (g) 7
           (d) F   (h) F   (d) 5   (h) 6

USING THE WORDS
(1) (a) revered   (f) divine
     (b) heresy   (g) interrogators
     (c) liberate   (h) heir
     (d) siege   (i) revelations
     (e) secular

SELECTION 9—THE BIGGEST CARRIER OF INF0RMATION
THINKING IT OVER
(1) The laser.
(2) *Any three of the following:* burning away warts and cancers; sealing blood vessels; repairing detached retinas; painlessly drilling teeth; cutting diamonds; lighting the ocean; studying air pollution; measuring long distances, such as the distance from earth to moon; detecting art frauds.
(3) It means that waves of light are parallel and of the same size and frequency—they fit closely next to one another and do not scatter in different directions.

STUDYING THE PASSAGE
(1) c   (2) (a) F   (e) T   (3) (a) 5   (e) 6   (4) b   (5) d
           (b) T   (f) T   (b) 3   (f) 7
           (c) T   (g) T   (c) 8   (g) 1
           (d) F   (h) T   (d) 2   (h) 4

USING THE WORDS
(1) (a) volume   (f) frauds
     (b) frequency   (g) detect
     (c) detached   (h) warts
     (d) scattering   (i) volume
     (e) transmitted

SELECTION 10—NATURE'S MISCHIEF MAKES MIRAGES
THINKING IT OVER
(1) They make things appear that are not there, and can cause accidents, shipwrecks, etc.
(2) A French scientist, Gaspard Monge.

STUDYING THE PASSAGE
(1) c   (2) (a) T   (e) F   (3) (a) 6   (e) 4   (4) c   (5) d
           (b) T   (f) T   (b) 5   (f) 8
           (c) F   (g) T   (c) 2   (g) 1
           (d) T   (h) T   (d) 7   (h) 3

USING THE WORDS
(1) (a) mirage   (d) deception
        illusion   (e) sorcerer
        hallucination   (f) density
     (b) phantom   (g) turreted
     (c) baffled

SELECTION 11—THE STRUGGLE FOR SURVIVAL
THINKING IT OVER
(1) The competition for survival between different organisms.
(2) The cat (also, the lizard that escaped, and those birds not attacked).

STUDYING THE PASSAGE
(1) b   (2) (a) T   (e) F   (3) (a) 3   (e) 5   (4) b   (5) a
           (b) F   (f) F   (b) 6   (f) 7
           (c) T   (g) T   (c) 2   (g) 1
           (d) T   (h) T   (d) 8   (h) 4

USING THE WORDS
(1) (a) wary   (f) degradation
     (b) alien   (g) glen
     (c) cunning   (h) alien
     (d) concept   (i) feline
     (e) haven

SELECTION 12—LIFE'S MYSTERY
THINKING IT OVER
(1) Water may have been the place where early molecules and compounds accumulated to develop into the first living cells.
(2) Such words show that scientists, even when experiments seem to say something is true, do not make positive statements of fact until they have absolute proof that they are correct.

STUDYING THE PASSAGE
(1) a   (2) (a) T   (e) F   (3) (a) 7   (e) 4   (4) d   (5) d
           (b) F   (f) T   (b) 8   (f) 1
           (c) T   (g) F   (c) 6   (g) 3
           (d) T   (h) T   (d) 5   (h) 2

USING THE WORDS
(1) (a) vigilance   (f) relentlessly
     (b) nucleus   (g) chromosomal
     (c) primitive   (h) osmosis
     (d) primitive   (i) diffusion
     (e) homeostatic   (j) primeval

SELECTION 13—WHERE'S THE MATTER?
THINKING IT OVER
(1) (a) The rate of expansion is decreasing, slowing down.
     (b) The gravitational attraction from matter.
     (c) There is not enough *visible* matter to account for such a great amount of gravity; black holes would supply the missing gravitational force.

STUDYING THE PASSAGE
(1) c   (2) (a) T   (e) F   (3) (a) 4   (e) 2   (4) c   (5) c
           (b) F   (f) T   (b) 7   (f) 3
           (c) T   (g) T   (c) 1   (g) 5
           (d) T   (h) T   (d) 8   (h) 6

USING THE WORDS
(1) (a) gravitational   (e) thermonuclear
     (b) propounded   (f) galaxy
     (c) condensed   (g) recesses
     (d) literally   (h) recesses

SELECTION 14—SYMBOLIC LOGIC
THINKING IT OVER
(1) All sardines can swim.
(2) It can be used as an aid in simple cases of deductive reasoning.
STUDYING THE PASSAGE
(1) d   (2) (a) T   (e) F   (3) (a) 7   (e) 3   (4) b, d   (5) c
           (b) T   (f) F   (b) 1   (f) 6
           (c) F   (g) T   (c) 8   (g) 5
           (d) F   (h) T   (d) 4   (h) 2
USING THE WORDS
(1) (a) argument   (f) hypothesis
    (b) valid   (g) premise
    (c) modify   (h) argument
    (d) disjointed   (i) inescapable
    (e) misgivings   (j) deduction

SELECTION 15—A PROBLEM IN LOGIC
THINKING IT OVER
(1) Ramona.
(2) A process of reasoning that draws a general conclusion about a class of objects or events when some members of the class (but not all) have been examined. (The important point is that this reasoning reaches a conclusion that is a *more* general statement than the statements or facts from which it is derived. This is the opposite of deductive reasoning.)
STUDYING THE PASSAGE
(1) b   (2) (a) F   (e) F   (3) (a) 4   (e) 3   (4) b   (5) c
           (b) T   (f) T   (b) 7   (f) 8
           (c) T   (g) F   (c) 5   (g) 2
           (d) F   (h) T   (d) 1   (h) 6
USING THE WORDS
(1) (a) induction
    (b) formula
    (c) programmer
    (d) instance
    (e) appropriate

(2) WRITING ABOUT IT

	livingroom	den	kitchen	bathroom	playroom
Stephanie	x	x	x	x	o
Ray	x	x	x	o	x
Stan	o	x	x	x	x
Charles	x	o	x	x	x
Bruce	x	x	o	x	x

SELECTION 16—TWO PASSAGES FROM THE BIBLE
THINKING IT OVER
(1) To love each other; to be loving.
(2) A short story (usually fictional) told to illustrate a moral or religious principle.
(3) Someone who helps others.
(4) The speaker's understanding of God now, in contrast to what he will understand some day, is likened to a child's understanding in comparison with an adult's.
(5) Today, charity commonly means generosity to the poor or needy. Verses 3–7, especially 3, show that Paul did not have such a narrow idea in mind.
STUDYING THE PASSAGE
(1) c   (2) (a) F   (e) T   (3) (a) 4   (e) 2   (4) c, d   (5) a
           (b) F   (f) T   (b) 7   (f) 5
           (c) T   (g) T   (c) 1   (g) 3
           (d) F   (h) T   (d) 8   (h) 6
USING THE WORDS
(1) (a) profound   (f) bestow
    (b) iniquity   (g) unseemly
    (c) compassion   (h) vaunteth
    (d) cymbal   (i) abideth
    (e) raiment

SELECTION 17—ANCIENT NUMERICAL CONCEPTS
THINKING IT OVER
(1) Because $1 + 2 + 3 + 4 = 10$.
(2) The first four numbers. They represented fire, water, air, and earth (all of the elements).
STUDYING THE PASSAGE
(1) b   (2) (a) T   (e) F   (3) (a) 4   (e) 3   (4) a   (5) a
           (b) F   (f) T   (b) 1   (f) 7
           (c) F   (g) F   (c) 6   (g) 2
           (d) T   (h) T   (d) 8   (h) 5
USING THE WORD
(1) (a) wavering   (e) correspondence
    (b) beneficent   (f) malevolent
    (c) ultimate   (g) factor
    (d) characteristics   (h) embody

SELECTION 18—HOW TO OUTWIT YOUR OPPONENT
THINKING IT OVER
(1) Game theory deals with events that are controllable by the players—events, therefore, that can be affected by strategy. Probability theory is concerned with games and situations that players have no control over, and in which the outcome is determined by chance alone, as in dice games.
(2) A randomized strategy prevents your opponent from knowing what you are going to do, since you yourself don't know what you are going to do. It, therefore, increases your chances of winning.
STUDYING THE PASSAGE
(1) b   (2) (a) F   (e) T   (3) (a) 4   (e) 8   (4) a, c   (5) a
           (b) T   (f) F   (b) 3   (f) 7
           (c) T   (g) T   (c) 2   (g) 6
           (d) F   (h) F   (d) 1   (h) 5
USING THE WORDS
(1) (a) bluff   (e) randomize
    (b) inferences   (f) scheme
    (c) innovative   (g) strategy
    (d) probability   (h) thwarting

SELECTION 19—THE MYSTERY OF DEATH
THINKING IT OVER
(1) The giant Owuo (a character like a god) controls life and death.
(2) Death continues forever, for all people.
(3) Young people have a strong desire to live; they are willing to take chances even when the result could be dangerous.
STUDYING THE PASSAGE
(1) a   (2) (a) F   (e) T   (3) (a) 4   (e) 8   (4) b   (5) b
           (b) T   (f) F   (b) 2   (f) 1
           (c) F   (g) F   (c) 5   (g) 6
           (d) F   (h) F   (d) 7   (h) 3
USING THE WORDS
(1) (a) famine   (e) proposed
    (b) bush   (f) presently
    (c) concealed   (g) compromise
    (d) stead

SELECTION 20—OZYMANDIAS
THINKING IT OVER
(1) A king of long ago who was very powerful and full of his own importance.
(2) The sculptor understood exactly the kind of man Ozymandias was—cruel, ruthless, and full of himself.
STUDYING THE PASSAGE
(1) c   (2) (a) T   (e) T   (3) (a) 7   (e) 6   (4) d   (5) a
           (b) T   (f) T   (b) 1   (f) 3
           (c) T   (g) F   (c) 4   (g) 5
           (d) T   (h) F   (d) 2

USING THE WORDS
(1) (a) antique   (f) sneer
    (b) visage   (g) sculptor
    (c) pedestal   (h) shattered
    (d) antique   (i) mocked
    (e) survive

SELECTION 21—KOKO'S HOME
THINKING IT OVER
(1) A mobile home or trailer.
(2) She is being studied.

STUDYING THE PASSAGE
(1) c   (2) (a) T (e) F   (3) (a) 6 (e) 8   (4) b, c (5) c
        (b) T (f) T   (b) 1 (f) 4
        (c) F (g) T   (c) 5 (g) 7
        (d) T (h) T   (d) 2 (h) 3

USING THE WORDS
(1) (a) abhors   (f) domain
    (b) monologue   (g) exclusively
    (c) plush   (h) gourmet
    (d) installation (i) roused
    (e) auditory

SELECTION 22—LOUISA MAY ALCOTT
THINKING IT OVER
(1) From her family and personal experiences.
(2) The second of the March sisters and a portrayal of Louisa herself.
(3) Louisa Alcott described the drawbacks in the appearance and nature of her heroine. What made this unusual was that Louisa was actually describing herself.

STUDYING THE PASSAGE
(1) d   (2) (a) F (e) T   (3) (a) 8 (e) 5   (4) a (5) a
        (b) T (f) F   (b) 2 (f) 6
        (c) F (g) F   (c) 7 (g) 4
        (d) T (h) T   (d) 3 (h) 1

USING THE WORDS
(1) (a) counterpart (f) autocratically
    (b) flattery   (g) semblance
    (c) fathom   (h) conventional
    (d) striking   (i) flattery
    (e) undertook

SELECTION 23—THE WALTZ
THINKING IT OVER
(1) b
(2) He is (a) boring, dull, difficult to talk to; (b) unattractive; (c) a terrible dancer.
(3) (a) Double-time Charlie or Swifty (b) He dances vigorously.
(4) A game of football.

STUDYING THE PASSAGE
(1) c   (2) (a) F (e) T   (3) (a) 4 (e) 6   (4) b (5) c
        (b) F (f) F   (b) 1 (f) 8
        (c) T (g) F   (c) 5 (g) 7
        (d) F (h) T   (d) 2 (h) 3

USING THE WORDS
(1) (a) acclimated   (f) noxious
    (b) premeditated (g) bestial
    (c) degenerate   (h) effete
    (d) gyrations   (i) maliciously
    (e) captious

SELECTION 24—THE MYSTERY OF MANDALAS
THINKING IT OVER
(1) Any three: To learn to draw; to make pleasant designs, including works of art; to express religious experience; to represent the unity of the universe and its relation to a human's soul; to express what is deepest in one's soul.
(2) Any three: the wheel; an eye; the face of a clock; a sign for a railroad crossing; a compass; stained-glass rose windows.

STUDYING THE PASSAGE
(1) b   (2) (a) F (e) F   (3) (a) 4 (e) 2   (4) a (5) c
        (b) T (f) F   (b) 8 (f) 5
        (c) T (g) F   (c) 7 (g) 1
        (d) T (h) T   (d) 6 (h) 3

USING THE WORDS
(1) (a) motif   (e) meditation
    (b) equinoxes   (f) symmetrical
    (c) coincidences (g) spontaneously
    (d) mystics

SELECTION 25—THE MYSTERIOUS POET: EMILY DICKINSON
THINKING IT OVER
(1) Early in her life Emily was very sociable; later she became a recluse.
(2) Any three of the following: nature, human experience, eternity, death, love and separation.
(3) Any three of the following: original metaphors, brilliant imagery, effective use of paradox, succinctness, portrayal of ordinary occurrences in fresh and striking ways.

STUDYING THE PASSAGE
(1) c   (2) (a) F (e) T   (3) (a) 6 (e) 2   (4) d (5) b
        (b) T (f) F   (b) 8 (f) 1
        (c) F (g) F   (c) 3 (g) 5
        (d) F (h) F   (d) 7 (h) 4

USING THE WORDS
(1) (a) apt   (f) ecstasy
    (b) precise   (g) lyric
    (c) paradox   (h) shunned
    (d) anguished (i) paisley
    (e) succinct

Printed in USA

ISBN 978-0-8388-9607-5

11 12 13 KSP 19

EDUCATORS PUBLISHING SERVICE
800.225.5750
www.epsbooks.com

This material belongs to:
Partners in Reading

ISBN 978-08388 9607-5

CONTENTS

subject: combined subjects

subject: social studies

subject: science

subject: philosophy, logic, and math

subject: literature and language

MYSTERY OF THE ANCIENT NAZCA LINES*

ABOUT THE PASSAGE   Strange, giant markings and designs can be found stretching for miles on the barren plateau of Peru. No one really knows how they got there or why they were made.

REASON FOR READING   To find out about these mysterious signs and some of the theories for their existence.

READ THE PASSAGE

For more than a mile, the desert in southern Peru has a curious ruler-straight and tack-sharp design made by rocks. The wandering mule paths that cross it only emphasize its precision.

Throughout hundreds of square miles of **arid** plateau, other such markings abound, most of them concentrated between the towns of Nazca and Palpa. Known as the Nazca Lines, they form a geometric **mélange** of **quadrangles**, triangles, and **trapezoids**. The markings also form spirals and flowers, narrow lines that extend more than five miles, and a desert zoo of giant creatures—birds, reptiles, whales, a monkey, and a spider—all made by stones whose patterns can only be seen from the air.

Because some of the figures resemble the ones that decorate Nazca pottery, **archaeologists attribute** the lines to the Nazcas, a coastal people whose culture rose, flourished, and declined between 100 B.C. and A.D. 700.

Making the patterns must have been extremely time-consuming. The Nazcas must have cleared millions of rocks to expose the lighter ground beneath them, piled the rocks in rows, and created designs that, in this nearly rainless region, can last thousands of years.

But why did they construct them? Nobody really knows. There have been many guesses. Some say that they were prehistoric roads, or farms. Others say they were signals or offerings to **celestial** beings. It has also been suggested that they constitute a giant **astronomical** calendar, an almanac for farmers who wished to predict the return of water to valley streams. One study did ascertain that some of the lines point to **solstice** positions of the sun and moon in ancient times, as well as to the rising and setting points on the horizon of some of the bright stars. But none of the theories have proven to be correct.

And so the mystery remains, including the most tantalizing question of all: why did the Nazcas create immense designs that they themselves could never see, designs that can only be seen from the air?

One person who worked to find out the answer was Maria Reiche. For over forty years she photographed and charted 'las lineas,' striving to complete a map of the hundreds of designs and figures of this area, which is some thirty miles long and threaded by the Pan American highway.

This determined German-born mathematician slept on a camp cot behind her car on the rocky, grassless Peruvian "pampa," and even when she was elderly, got up before daylight to conduct her research.

She scorned the suggestion that the markings may have been airfields for outer-space visitors to earth during prehistoric times. "Once you remove the stones, the ground is quite soft," she said. "I'm afraid the spacemen would have gotten stuck."

*From "Mystery of the Ancient Nazca Lines" by Loren McIntyre in *National Geographic Magazine,* vol. 147, no. 5, May 1975. Reprinted by permission of the National Geographic Society.

*In this sample selection, some answers to the questions are omitted so students can answer them.

Although Maria Reiche was not able to find the answer, she crusaded to preserve the patterns so that others following her might have a chance to do so.

THINKING IT OVER

(1) Give three theories suggested for the meaning and existence of the markings.

Prehistoric roads, farms, signals or offerings to celestial beings; a giant

astronomical calendar for farmers; airfields for outer-space visitors to earth.

(2) Who is thought to have created these unusual designs?

(3) Why do archaeologists believe that these people made the lines?

STUDYING THE PASSAGE

(1) Find the Main Idea: Choose one answer.
   (a) How strange designs on the Peruvian desert are being investigated.
   (b) How strange designs on the Peruvian desert are being preserved.
   (c) How strange designs on the Peruvian desert came into existence.
   (d) The mystery of strange designs on the Peruvian desert.   _d_

(2) Find the Facts: Mark each one *true* or *false*.
   (a) Mule paths have destroyed some of the designs.   (a) _F_
   (b) Some of the designs were in the shape of animals.   (b) _T_
   (c) The Nazcas lived between 100 B.C. and A.D. 700.   (c) ____
   (d) The markings took a long time to make.   (d) ____
   (e) The designs were visible only from the air.   (e) ____
   (f) Maria Reiche made a map of the designs.   (f) ____
   (g) Maria Reiche spent most of her life studying the designs. (g) ____
   (h) Maria Reiche camped out while doing her research.   (h) ____

(3) Find the Order: Number the following in the order in which they appear in the passage.
   (a) They form a geometrical mélange of quadrangles, triangles, and trapezoids. (a) _2_
   (b) She crusaded to preserve the lines.   (b) ____
   (c) The curious markings were ruler-straight and tack-sharp and more than a mile long. (c) ____
   (d) One person who tried to find out the answer was Maria Reiche.   (d) ____
   (e) They were coastal people whose culture rose, flourished, and declined.   (e) ____
   (f) She got up before daylight to do her research.   (f) ____
   (g) You have the designs that, in this nearly rainless region, can last thousands of years. (g) ____
   (h) Buy why did the ancients construct them?   (h) ____

(4) Go beyond the Facts: Which *one* of the following could you *not* conclude?
   (a) Many people must have been involved in the construction of the designs.
   (b) The people who created the designs must have had some knowledge of mathematics.
   (c) The people who created the designs must have had some artistic sense.
   (d) The people who created the designs did not mind working in the desert heat.   _d_

(5) Determine the Writer's Style and Technique: Which *one* of the following techniques does the writer use?

    (a) She presents an argument.

    (b) She gives a logical solution to a problem.

    (c) She gives a series of facts to explain something.

    (d) She gives a moving description.   _____

USING THE WORDS

(1) Words and Their Meanings: Find the boldfaced word for these definitions.

    quadrangles   (a) four-sided figures with four angles

    _____   (b) four-sided figures with two parallel sides

    _____   (c) to assign a cause to

    _____   (d) dry, barren

    _____   (e) to do with the sky, heavenly bodies

    _____   (f) mixture, medley

    _____   (g) to do with the stars

    _____   (h) scientists who study past human life and activities

    _____   (i) the shortest day of the year and the longest day of the year, occurring in winter and summer respectively

(2) Write a paragraph using three of the vocabulary words. Use a separate piece of paper.

WRITING ABOUT IT

Use a separate piece of paper.

(1) Reread the passage. Look for the topic sentences and main points, and underline them in one color. Note the facts and details and underline them in another color. Then make an outline of the passage.

(2) Try your hand at solving the Nazca Lines mystery. Make up a story that explains how the stories got there and why they are there.

Selection 2—Subject: Combined Subjects
Theme: Communication

CONVERSATIONS WITH A GORILLA*

ABOUT THE PASSAGE — Can animals communicate and use language the way humans do? This passage is about a gorilla who was taught to talk.**

REASON FOR READING — To find out more about the mystery of how humans and animals communicate.

READ THE PASSAGE

Researchers have successfully taught several chimpanzees to communicate with sign language, but Koko was the first gorilla to achieve **proficiency.**

Through the mastery of sign language, a means of communication used by the hearing impaired, she learned to communicate on a variety of subjects.

During the first six years that Francine "Penny" Patterson taught Koko, she estimated that Koko acquired a working vocabulary of approximately 375 signs that she used regularly and appropriately. They include such **diverse** words as: *airplane, belly button, lollipop, friend,* and *stethoscope.* However, because Penny talked to Koko while making the signs and hand gestures, Koko actually understood many more spoken words. In fact she became so proficient that **tantalizing** words such as *gum* and *candy* had to be spelled out in her presence.

What made Koko's accomplishment so impressive is that she not only could give the correct name to things, she could actually use language to express thoughts and feelings. This characteristic has traditionally been considered uniquely human.

She could ask and respond to a question, tell Penny when she felt happy or sad, and even show **empathy** toward others. Once when she saw a horse with a bit in its mouth, she signed, "Horse sad." When asked why the horse was sad she signed, "teeth." She was shown a photo of a famous gorilla, Snowflake, struggling against having a bath. Koko, who also hates baths, signed, "Me cry there," while pointing to the picture.

Koko also used language to express an impish sense of humor or to try to outwit her human companions. When asked the color of a white towel she replied, "Red." When told, "You know better, Koko. What color is it?" She insisted that it was "Red, Red, RED." Finally grinning broadly, she held up a minute speck of red lint that had been clinging to the towel. She seemed to **relish** the effects of her practical jokes, often responding exactly opposite to what she was asked to do. One day during a videotaping session, she was asked to place a toy animal under a bag. She responded by taking the toy and deliberately holding it above her head.

Koko also delighted in insulting her human friends, using such terms as *rotten stink, dirty, toilet, bird,* and *nut.* One day in a fit of **pique** she referred to Penny as a "toilet dirty devil." And on more than one occasion she has accurately described herself as a "stubborn devil."

Another characteristic of human language that Koko acquired was displacement—the ability to refer to events removed in time and place from the act of communication. For example, when Penny showed Koko the mark of a bite she had made earlier and asked, "You admit it?" Koko replied, "Sorry–bite, scratch." The most telling evidence that she could displace events was seen in her

*The facts in this selection were taken from "Conversations with a Gorilla," by Francine Patterson. *National Geographic Magazine*, vol. 154, no. 4, October 1978. Used by permission of the National Geographic Society.

**Those interested in more information about Koko can visit the Gorilla Foundations online @ www.gorilla.org

lying. For when someone tells a lie, they use language to **distort** the listener's **perception** of reality. The person uses symbols to describe something that never happened or will not happen. Koko discovered the value of a lie to avoid "getting in trouble" at the age of five. One of her first lies was when she blamed Penny's assistant for breaking a sink that she, Koko, sat on.

Some of her lies were startlingly ingenious, such as pretending to use her crayon as a lipstick when accused of chewing on it.

Koko could acquire signs that refer to past and future. She could signal "first" and "later," and even learned to use the sign "later" to postpone discussion of possibly unpleasant subjects.

She also understood other words referring to the future. On a bright morning that followed weeks of rain, Penny told Koko that if it were still sunny during the afternoon she would take her out. When Penny arrived at three o'clock, Koko looked out at the still-bright weather and collected her gear to go outside.

Over the years, Koko's language became more flexible and sophisticated, so that she could define objects. When Penny asked her what a stove is she pointed to the stove and said, "Cook with." When asked, "What is an orange?" she replied, "Food, drink." She also gave a good definition of herself. When asked, "Are you an animal or a person?" her response was, "Fine animal, gorilla."

THINKING IT OVER

(1) How was Koko taught to talk? _____

_____

(2) How many signs could Koko use regularly and appropriately after six years of lessons?

_____

(3) What was so impressive about Koko's "speaking" accomplishments?

_____

_____

_____

STUDYING THE PASSAGE

(1) Find the Main Idea: Choose one answer.
   (a) How Koko learned to talk.
   (b) How Koko enjoyed using words.
   (c) How Koko's use of language was similar to that of humans.
   (d) How Koko liked to tease her human companions.   _____

(2) Find the Facts: Mark each one *true* or *false*.
   (a) Koko was the first gorilla to learn to use language effectively.   (a) _____
   (b) Penny talked to Koko when teaching her the signs for words.   (b) _____
   (c) Koko did not understand what sadness means.   (c) _____
   (d) Koko had a good sense of humor.   (d) _____
   (e) Displacement means the ability to refer to events removed in time and place
       from the act of communication.   (e) _____
   (f) Koko learned to lie right away.   (f) _____
   (g) Koko could tell past and future.   (g) _____
   (h) Koko had not learned to define objects.   (h) _____

(3) Find the Order: Number the following in the order in which they appear in the passage.
   (a) Penny showed Koko the mark of a bite she had made earlier. (a) _____
   (b) Penny told Koko that if it were still sunny during the afternoon she would
       take her out. (b) _____
   (c) Seeing a horse with a bit in its mouth, she signed, "Horse sad." (c) _____
   (d) Tantalizing words such as *gum* and *candy* had to be spelled out in her presence. (d) _____
   (e) When asked, "What is an orange?" she replied, "Food, drink." (e) _____
   (f) Koko was the first gorilla to achieve proficiency. (f) _____
   (g) Koko delighted in insulting her human friends. (g) _____
   (h) She insisted it was "Red, Red, RED." (h) _____

(4) Go beyond the Facts: Koko could communicate easily with which *one* of the following?
   (a) A blind person.
   (b) A hearing impaired person.
   (c) Someone speaking words.
   (d) Someone speaking a foreign language. _____

(5) Determine the Writer's Style and Technique: Which *one* of the following does the writer do?
   (a) She describes what Koko looks like.
   (b) She describes only her language achievements.
   (c) She describes a number of her achievements.
   (d) She tells you about the kind of life she leads. _____

USING THE WORDS

(1) Words and Their Meanings: Find the boldfaced word for these definitions.

   _____ (a) enjoy a great deal

   _____ (b) annoyance, irritation

   _____ (c) change, twist out of shape

   _____ (d) tempting

   _____ (e) great skill, expertness

   _____ (f) awareness, observation; discernment

   _____ (g) different, unlike

   _____ (h) understanding of another's feelings

(2) Write a paragraph using three of the words from the list above. Use a separate piece of paper.

WRITING ABOUT IT

Use a separate piece of paper.

(1) Write an interview that might take place between a television commentator and Penny Patterson. Write your questions and answers in dialogue form; just as though they are talking on a talk show.

(2) What is your opinion on animal rights? For example, subjecting animals, such as the gorilla, Koko, to experiments, such as the one described in the passage? Do you think animals should be used in any experiments, even if the research benefits humans?

THE ONLY WAY TO TRAVEL*

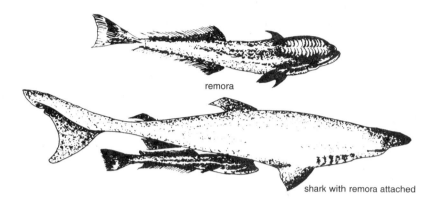

remora

shark with remora attached

ABOUT THE PASSAGE   Depending on others is necessary for many creatures; for some it is even a way of life.

REASON FOR READING   To follow a logical presentation of facts.

READ THE PASSAGE

Where you live, chances are there are laws against hitchhiking. If not, most people would agree that it is unwise to get a ride from a passing motorist. In the animal and plant world, however, hitchhiking is encouraged by nature's laws.

Many animals regularly depend on larger creatures for transportation. Plants, anchored to the soil, use clever devices to make certain their pollen and seeds get a free ride to a spot where they can take root.

One of the most efficient hitchhikers among animals is the remora, or shark sucker. With a suction disk on top of its head, it attaches itself to a shark, marlin, or barracuda. The passenger takes nourishment as it rides along, feeding on tidbits from the meals of its living host.

Barnacles swim free when they are young. Later, however, they attach themselves permanently to an object, frequently the bottom of a ship or whale, and with it take **excursions** to the farthest reaches of the oceans.

Tiny **aquatic** snails living in the Florida Everglades prefer air travel. They have extended their range to South America by cruising comfortably **aloft** in the feathers of a bird, the ibis.

Perhaps the smallest stowaways are mites, who hitch a ride on hummingbirds. No bigger than twice the size of the period at the end of this sentence, these creatures have no eyes, relying on sensitive body bristles and a keen sense of smell to guide them through life. But they are smart. They use the hummingbird to take them from flower to flower to gather the sugar-rich nectar they need to live on.

Some flying creatures also look for free rides to distant places. One tiny fly makes long-distance flights without expending a bit of energy. Its preferred **mode** of transportation is flying attached to the back of a night-flying beetle.

Sea birds have been seen cruising on the backs of big pelicans and turtles. Land birds, such as starlings, have crossed the ocean as uninvited

*From "The Old Explorer: Animal Hitchhikers," *National Geographic School Bulletin,* vol. 41, no. 2, October 8, 1962. Reprinted by permission of the *National Geographic School Bulletin.*

guests on ships, which are also used as resting grounds by weary **migrant** birds. The albatross, who covers amazing distances as it travels in a continuous, easterly circle around Antarctica, catches a ride on the easterly winds.

Plants also travel as chance stowaways on ships, springing up wherever **ballast** and cargoes are unloaded. But deliberate hitchhiking by plants is more involved. Many flowering plants rely on **cross-pollination,** either by wind or insects. Trusting the wind is risky, so nature, through **evolution,** has created such devices as the spines on cockleburrs, the hooks on Spanish needles, the triangles on tick-trefoil, and the gummy substance on beggar's lice. These plant devices fasten onto animal or human passersby and ride to a new home.

In the South Pacific, gluey seeds of the pisonia stick to the feathers of birds. Occasionally, a bird becomes so encrusted with seeds that it cannot fly.

Plants demonstrated their remarkable ability to travel after the volcanic eruption of Krakatau in 1883. The explosion killed every living thing on the Indonesian island. Yet, in ten years, the barren isle was again covered with vegetation.

THINKING IT OVER

(1) List four ways that creatures mentioned in the passage travel without using their own energy.

  (a) _____

  (b) _____

  (c) _____

  (d) _____

(2) List three ways plants transport their seeds or pollen.

  (a) _____

  (b) _____

  (c) _____

STUDYING THE PASSAGE

(1) Find the Main Idea: Choose one answer.
  (a) How creatures travel.
  (b) Why hitchhiking should be allowed in the United States.
  (c) What we can learn from nature.
  (d) How nature provides a means of travel for some of the world's inhabitants.   _____

(2) Find the Facts: Mark each one *true* or *false*.
  (a) A certain snail attaches itself to an ibis.   (a) _____
  (b) Plants have clever devices to transport their pollen and seeds to new growing spots. (b) _____
  (c) Some seeds are gluey.   (c) _____
  (d) Barnacles attach themselves to sharks for a free ride.   (d) _____
  (e) Spines on cockleburrs are nature's protection against insects.   (e) _____
  (f) Krakatau erupted in 1956.   (f) _____
  (g) Starlings have stowed away on ships crossing the ocean.   (g) _____
  (h) The wind destroys plant pollen.   (h) _____

(3) Find the Order: Number the following in the order in which they appear in the passage.
  (a) Sea birds sometimes cruise on the backs of turtles. (a) _____
  (b) The remora rides on a shark, marlin, or barracuda. (b) _____
  (c) Ten years after Krakatau erupted, the Indonesian island was covered with vegetation. (c) _____
  (d) Barnacles sometimes attach themselves to a whale. (d) _____
  (e) Cross-pollination relies on wind or insects. (e) _____
  (f) Beggar's lice has a gummy substance. (f) _____
  (g) There are probably laws against hitchhiking where you live. (g) _____
  (h) Night-flying beetles sometimes give tiny flies a ride. (h) _____

(4) Go beyond the Facts: Which *one* can you conclude from the passage?
  (a) Children who hitchhike put themselves in danger.
  (b) Animals hitchhike because they don't know any better.
  (c) People who hitchhike might be following nature's way.
  (d) Plants should be prevented from hitchhiking by strict laws. _____

(5) Determine the Writer's Style and Technique: Choose two answers.
  (a) She suggests various science projects.
  (b) She develops one idea through many examples.
  (c) She groups related kinds of examples together.
  (d) She uses animals and plants to explain human behavior. _____ _____

USING THE WORDS

(1) Words and Their Meanings: Find the boldfaced word for these definitions.

  _____ (a) growing or living in water

  _____ (b) method, way, style

  _____ (c) trips

  _____ (d) transfer of pollen from one flower to another by wind or insects

  _____ (e) moving periodically from one place to another to live or work

  _____ (f) up in the air, high above the ground

  _____ (g) any heavy substance used in a ship to improve stability

  _____ (h) a process of development or gradual change.

(2) Write a paragraph using three of the words from the list above. Use a separate piece of paper.

WRITING ABOUT IT

Use a separate piece of paper.

(1) Describe the different ways creatures move around with no effort on their part.

(2) Describe in detail an especially interesting journey you have been on.

WILLIAMSBURG, VIRGINIA

ABOUT THE PASSAGE

The small town of Williamsburg is very similar today to what it was 200 years ago. You can see horsedrawn carriages, a candlemaker toiling over a hot vat, and people strolling down the street in long dresses and britches. How do you think it has remained so quaint? (a) The people secluded themselves from neighboring towns; (b) the Amish people live there; (c) the town became a quiet, little country town; years after, it was historically restored.

REASON FOR READING

As you read this selection, look for the historical facts that show the changing role of Williamsburg in America.

READ THE PASSAGE

Williamsburg, Virginia is a peaceful town. It has a village green, **cobblestone** streets, formal gardens filled with flowers, and attractive colonial architecture. The village has been restored to look just as it did during colonial times, some 200 years ago.

Today you can stroll past reconstructed craft shops, look at the brightly-painted signs, and ride in horse-drawn carriages. There is a feeling of peace, but Williamsburg has not always been tranquil. The monuments remind you that the **militia** drilled on the green, the wounded were carried along the cobblestones, and many decisions that affected the course of American history were made there.

Williamsburg was the capital of Virginia from 1699 to 1779; one of this country's first colleges, William and Mary, is located there. This small southern town was also once the home of our country's most **radical** legislators. It was in 1765, in Williamsburg, in the House of Burgesses that Patrick Henry delivered his famous speech. He attacked the British government and its king; he decried the Stamp Act with the words: "Caesar had his Brutus, Charles the First his Cromwell, and George the Third may profit by their example!" The **implication** of these words was that George the Third could be overthrown by America just as Caesar had been overthrown by Brutus, and Charles had been overthrown by

Cromwell. In spite of the cries of **treason** from some legislators, Mr. Henry prevailed; the seeds of **revolution** had been sown.

During the next ten years, Williamsburg was a center for the growth of revolutionary sentiment within the southern colonies, just as Boston was a center within the New England colonies. Not long after he made his famous speech, Patrick Henry began to meet with Thomas Jefferson, George Washington, George Wythe, George Mason, and other patriots. The Raleigh Tavern in Williamsburg was the location of their secret meetings.

In 1776, the original version of our Bill of Rights and Constitution were drafted in Williamsburg, which became a headquarters for the Americans during the Revolutionary War. At that time, wounded soldiers were **quartered** in the Governor's Palace. But in 1780, as the Revolutionary War was ending, the capital of Virginia moved to Richmond, where it has since remained. Williamsburg was no longer a center for new ideas and legislation; almost immediately it was transformed into a small country town. The famous statesmen moved away, businesses declined or died out, and the population of the town **dwindled.**

As you wander down the streets of Williamsburg today and look into the quaint shops to watch a costumed weaver working steadily at the loom, or a candlemaker toiling over hot vats, or a baker twisting dough into oddly shaped loaves, you can easily imagine yourself back in the town of 200 years ago. Admittedly, there are other tourists, but somehow they fade into the background. This is because the restoration has been so skillfully completed that the town's historical atmosphere **pervades** everything.

The restoration began in 1926, thanks to William Goodwin, who interested John D. Rockefeller in the project. At the cost of $62,000,000 some 600 modern structures were taken down and about 500 buildings were reconstructed on their original sites. Whenever possible old architectural plans were copied so that many buildings are exact replicas of their originals.

Thus, the Williamsburg of today looks very much like the Williamsburg of yesterday. Now, however, it is not a center of **dissent**, but a living museum of American history.

THINKING IT OVER

(1) What did Patrick Henry mean when he said: "George the Third may profit by their example"?

_____

_____

(2) State the present and past role of Williamsburg in America. _____

_____

_____

STUDYING THE PASSAGE

(1) Find the Main Idea: Choose one answer.
   (a) Williamsburg was the colonial capital of Virginia.
   (b) The real significance of Williamsburg is contained not in its restored buildings but rather in the ideas of the people who congregated there during the Revolutionary period.
   (c) Williamsburg would be a nice place to visit if you like seeing old things that have been restored.
   (d) Wounded soldiers were quartered in the Governor's Palace in Williamsburg during the Revolutionary War. _____

(2) Find the Facts: Mark each one *true* or *false*.
   (a) Williamsburg was moved to Richmond in 1780. (a) _____
   (b) William and Mary are a famous southern couple who founded Williamsburg. (b) _____
   (c) Williamsburg once housed America's most radical legislators. (c) _____
   (d) The Raleigh Tavern was the location of secret meetings that were attended by Patrick Henry, Thomas Jefferson, George Washington, George Wythe, and others. (d) _____
   (e) About $62,000,000 was spent on the restoration of Williamsburg. (e) _____
   (f) After the Revolutionary War the town of Williamsburg became a huge city. (f) _____
   (g) About 600 buildings were taken down and 500 were reconstructed during the restoration of Williamsburg. (g) _____
   (h) Williamsburg is still known for its new and daring political ideas. (h) _____

11

(3) Find the Order: Number the following in the order in which they appear in the passage.
  (a) Monuments remind you that the militia once drilled on the green. (a) _____
  (b) Many buildings are exact replicas of the originals. (b) _____
  (c) Williamsburg, Virginia is a peaceful town. (c) _____
  (d) This town once housed America's most radical legislators. (d) _____
  (e) Williamsburg was a revolutionary center in the southern colonies. (e) _____
  (f) Williamsburg is now a living museum. (f) _____
  (g) Patrick Henry delivered his famous revolutionary speech. (g) _____
  (h) The famous statesmen moved away, businesses declined or died out, and the population dwindled. (h) _____

(4) Go beyond the Facts: Choose one answer.
  (a) Revolutions often result from secret meetings held in small-town taverns.
  (b) The first people to become angry and dissatisfied enough to start a revolution are the people in colleges.
  (c) Revolution is often necessary to free people from oppressive governments that do not represent them; however, as the American Revolution shows, it is a very risky, and often bloody, way of changing things.
  (d) Revolutions may be exciting, but they are always started by a group of radical, destructive people who are out to replace the establishment with anarchy. _____

(5) Determine the Writer's Style and Technique: Choose one answer.
  (a) The author presents mainly factual and historical information.
  (b) The author writes historical fiction.
  (c) The author focuses on Williamsburg's beauty.
  (d) The author compares two important colonial towns. _____

USING THE WORDS

(1) Words and Their Meanings: Find the boldfaced word for these definitions.

_____ (a) a naturally rounded stone larger than a pebble and smaller than a boulder

_____ (b) people in emergency military service

_____ (c) a statement that indicates a relationship between two things and from which a conclusion may be drawn

_____ (d) the offense of attempting, by one's actions, to overthrow a government or state to which one owes allegiance

_____ (e) a complete change in government, usually by overthrowing a government already in existence

_____ (f) provided with lodging or shelter

_____ (g) became steadily less, shrank

_____ (h) difference of opinion, especially disagreement with the political opinions of the majority

_____ (i) inclined to make extreme changes in existing ways

_____ (j) spreads through everything

12

(2) Write a paragraph using three of the words from the list above. Use a separate piece of paper.

WRITING ABOUT IT

Use a separate piece of paper.

(1) Using the facts from the passage, combined with any research you can do and your imagination, describe what you think Williamsburg was like during the period from 1699 to 1779.

(2) In his speech, Patrick Henry expressed strong feelings about American opposition to the British. What do you feel strongly about? Write a speech to be delivered to the class on an issue you care about. Be sure to state your main points clearly, and give specific examples and facts to back up these points.

JOHN F. KENNEDY'S INAUGURAL ADDRESS

ABOUT THE PASSAGE   John F. Kennedy was one of the most charismatic presidents the United States has had. He was especially adept at delivering speeches that roused the enthusiasm of his listeners. Notice how well he does this in his famous inaugural address.

REASON FOR READING   To notice Kennedy's effective use of language to express his ideas, and to understand his message.

READ THE PASSAGE

" . . . Let the word go forth from this time and place, to friend and foe alike, that the torch has been passed to a new generation of Americans—born in this century, **tempered** by war, **disciplined** by a hard and bitter peace, proud of our ancient heritage—and unwilling to witness or permit slow undoing of those human rights to which this nation has always been **committed**, and to which we are committed today at home and around the world. . . .

In your hands, my fellow citizens, more than mine, will rest the final success or failure of our course. Since this country was founded, each generation of Americans has been **summoned** to give **testimony** to its national loyalty. The graves of young Americans who answered the call to service surround the globe.

Now the trumpet summons us again—not as a call to bear arms, though arms we need—not as a call to battle, though embattled we are—but a call to hear the **burden** of a long twilight struggle, year in and year out, "rejoicing in hope, patient in tribulation"—a struggle against the common enemies of man: **tyranny**, poverty, disease, and war itself. . . .

In the long history of the world, only a few generations have been granted the role of defending freedom in its hour of maximum danger. I do not shrink from this responsibility—I welcome it. I do not believe that any of us would exchange places with any other people or any other generation. The energy, the faith, the devotion which we bring to this **endeavor** will light our country and all who serve it—and the glow from that fire can truly light the world.

And so, my fellow Americans: ask not what your country can do for you—ask what you can do for your country. . . . "

THINKING IT OVER

(1) What is the main message or challenge in John F. Kennedy's speech? _____

_____

_____

_____

(2) What does the torch stand for? _____

_____

_____

_____

(3) What does the trumpet call bring to mind? _____

_____

_____

(4) Why does Kennedy use the phrases "my fellow citizens" and "my fellow Americans"? _____

_____

STUDYING THE PASSAGE

(1) Find the Main Idea: Choose one answer.
   (a) Each person must find ways to fight against tyranny, poverty, disease and war itself.
   (b) The torch of the Statue of Liberty shines in New York harbor.
   (c) Human rights have been guaranteed by history.
   (d) Too many young Americans already have been buried by war. _____

(2) Find the Facts: Mark each one *true* or *false*.
   (a) The speech is meant to concern people about other people's rights as well
       as their own. (a) _____
   (b) The new generation of Americans is too inexperienced to help its country. (b) _____
   (c) The success or failure of the struggle for American ideals rests with the
       president alone. (c) _____
   (d) The trumpet does not summon us to bear arms. (d) _____
   (e) We are called to bear the burden of a long twilight struggle. (e) _____
   (f) The common enemies of all people are tyranny, poverty, disease, and war itself. (f) _____
   (g) Kennedy was aware of the danger facing America. (g) _____
   (h) Kennedy said that it was the government's responsibility to defend freedom. (h) _____

(3) Find the Order: Number the following in the order in which they appear in the passage.
   (a) Americans today are committed to upholding human rights at home and abroad. (a) _____
   (b) Every generation since America was founded has been called upon to
       show its loyalty. (b) _____
   (c) This generation will fight against war itself. (c) _____
   (d) Friends and enemies must hear this message. (d) _____
   (e) Americans must seek ways to serve their country. (e) _____
   (f) All over the world, young Americans have died serving their country. (f) _____
   (g) The struggle facing us will be a long one. (g) _____
   (h) A new generation has learned the hard way—from history, from peace,
       and from war. (h) _____

(4) Go beyond the Facts: After reading this passage, we can conclude which *one*
   of the following?
   (a) Americans should know their own history better.
   (b) There have been too many wars.
   (c) Each American is responsible for the welfare of the nation.
   (d) Modern technology will soon solve the world's age-old problems. _____

(5) Determine the Writer's Style and Technique: Choose one answer.
    (a) Makes many grand promises.
    (b) Makes the listener feel involved with national ideals.
    (c) Develops one idea thoroughly by giving facts.
    (d) Outlines his legislative plans.   _____

USING THE WORDS

(1) Words and Their Meanings: Find the boldfaced word for these definitions. One word has *two* meanings.

_____   (a) called upon

_____   (b) an effort to do something; an undertaking

_____   (c) a statement used for proof; evidence

_____   (d) trained; controlled; given will power

_____   (e) a heavy load

_____   (f) dedicated or pledged

_____   (g) made stronger and more resilient; toughened

_____   (h) the cruel or unjust use of power; a government by an absolute ruler

_____   (i) moderated; made less harsh by the addition of some other ingredient

WRITING ABOUT IT

Use a separate piece of paper.

(1) Describe the ways you think you and your friends can help your country.

(2) Write a speech on an issue or topic that is important to you. Try to make your language as effective as possible in conveying your thoughts and feelings. Try out different word combinations and phrasing. Read your speech out loud to a classmate.

Selection 6—Subject: Social Studies
Theme: Human Relations

JO'S SACRIFICE*

ABOUT THE PASSAGE   Louisa May Alcott wrote *Little Women* in 1868. At that time many values, attitudes, and customs were different from those of today. The lasting popularity of the novel shows, however, that certain values such as love and sacrifice for one's family are still important in today's society.

REASON FOR READING   To find out what Jo did to help her family.

READ THE PASSAGE

The March family was a close one. When word arrived that Mr. March, a Civil War army chaplain, was very ill, Mrs. March wanted to go to him at once. But she didn't have the money and could not figure out how to get it. Her four daughters were upset by their father's condition, their mother's **predicament**, and their seeming helplessness. Then Jo, the second oldest, came up with a solution:

She came walking in with a very queer expression, for there was a mixture of fun and fear, satisfaction and regret in it, which puzzled the family as much as did the rolls of bills she laid before her mother, saying with a little choke in her voice "That's my contribution toward making father comfortable and bringing him home!"

"My dear, where did you get it? Twenty-five dollars! Jo, I hope you haven't done anything **rash**?"

"No, it's mine honestly; I didn't beg, borrow, or steal it. I earned it; and I don't think you'll blame me, for I only sold what was my own."

As she spoke, Jo took off her bonnet, and a general outcry arose, for all her abundant hair was cut short.

"Your hair! Your beautiful hair! O Jo, how could you? Your one beauty. My dear girl, there as no need of this. She doesn't look like my Jo any more, but I love her dearly for it!"

As everyone exclaimed, and Beth hugged the **cropped** head tenderly, Jo **assumed** an **indifferent air**, which did not deceive anyone a particle, and said, rumpling up the brown bush, and trying to look

as if she liked it, "It doesn't affect the fate of the nation, so don't wail, Beth. It will be good for my **vanity**; I was getting too proud of my wig. It will do my brains good to have that mop taken off; my head feels deliciously light and cool, and the barber said I could soon have a curly crop, which will be boyish, becoming, and easy to keep in order. I'm satisfied; so please take the money, and let's have supper."

"Tell me all about it, Jo. *I* am not quite satisfied, but I can't blame you, for I know how willingly you sacrificed your vanity, as you call it, to your love. But, my dear, it was not necessary, and I'm afraid you will regret it, one of these days," said Mrs. March.

"No, I won't!" returned Jo stoutly, feeling much relieved that her prank was not entirely **condemned**.

"What made you do it?" asked Amy, who would as soon have thought of cutting off her head as her pretty hair.

"Well, I was wild to do something for father," replied Jo, as they gathered about the table.

"I hate to borrow as much as mother does, and I knew Aunt March would croak; she always does, if you ask for a ninepence. Meg gave all her quarterly salary toward the rent, and I only got some clothes with mine, so I felt wicked, and was bound to have some money, if I sold the nose off my face to get it."

"You needn't feel wicked, my child: you had no winter things, and got the simplest with your own hard earnings," said Mrs. March, with a look that warmed Jo's heart.

"I hadn't the least idea of selling my hair at first, but as I went along I kept thinking

*From *Little Women* by Louisa May Alcott. Originally published by Little, Brown & Company.

17

what I could do, and feeling as if I'd like to dive into some of the rich stores and help myself. In a barber's window I saw tails of hair with the prices marked; and one black tail, not so thick as mine, was forty dollars. It came over me all of a sudden that I had one thing to make money out of, and without stopping to think, I walked in, asked if they bought hair, and what they would give for mine."

"I don't see how you dared to do it," said Beth, in a tone of **awe**.

"Oh, he was a little man who looked as if he merely lived to oil his hair. He rather stared, at first, as if he wasn't used to having girls bounce into his shop and ask him to buy their hair. He said he didn't care about mine, it wasn't the fashionable color, and he never paid much for it in the first place; the work put into it made it dear, and so on. It was getting late, and I was afraid, if it wasn't done right away, that I shouldn't have it done at all, and you know when I start to do a thing, I hate to give it up; so I begged him to take it, and told him why I was in such a hurry. It was silly, I dare say, but it changed his mind, for I got rather excited, and told the story in my topsy-turvy way, and his wife heard, and said so kindly:"'Take it, Thomas, and **oblige** the young lady; I'd do as much for our Jimmy any day if I had a spire[1] of hair worth selling.'"

[1]coil

THINKING IT OVER

(1) A major fuss is made over Jo's cutting her hair. Would people react the same way or differently today? Explain. _____

_____

_____

_____

_____

_____

(2) What does Jo's act show about her feeling for her father? _____

_____

_____

STUDYING THE PASSAGE

(1) Find the Main Idea: Choose one answer.
   (a) What to do if your family needs money.
   (b) How to lose your hair.
   (c) How Jo angered her family.
   (d) What Jo did for her family.   _____

(2) Find the Facts: Mark each of these *true* or *false*.
   (a) Jo had mixed feelings about losing her hair.   (a) _____
   (b) Jo got forty dollars for her hair.   (b) _____
   (c) Jo had been proud of her hair.   (c) _____
   (d) It was evening when Jo came home.   (d) _____
   (e) Mrs. March was cross with Jo for what she did.   (e) _____
   (f) The family needed money.   (f) _____
   (g) Jo had a job.   (g) _____
   (h) Jo had to beg the barber to cut her hair.   (h) _____

18

(3) Find the Order: Number the following in the order in which they appear in the passage.

(a) "Meg gave all her quarterly salary toward the rent." (a) _____

(b) "I saw tails of hair with the prices marked." (b) _____

(c) She came walking in with a queer expression. (c) _____

(d) "Your hair! Your beautiful hair!" (d) _____

(e) "He was a little man who looked as if he merely lived to oil his hair." (e) _____

(f) "I was getting too proud of my wig." (f) _____

(g) "What made you do it?" asked Amy. (g) _____

(h) "I got rather excited and told the story in my topsy-turvy way." (h) _____

(4) Go beyond the Facts: Which words best describe Jo? Look up the words if you do not know their meanings.

(a) Foolish.

(b) Loving.

(c) Unselfish.

(d) Headstrong.

(e) Greedy.

_____ _____ _____

(5) Determine the Writer's Style and Technique: What *three* methods does the writer use to make the characters in her story seem real?

(a) She describes their behavior.

(b) She has the father describe them.

(c) She shows their feelings.

(d) She quotes their exact words.

_____ _____ _____

USING THE WORDS

(1) Words and Their Meanings: Find the boldfaced word for these definitions.

_____ (a) declared to be wrong or bad

_____ (b) outward appearance

_____ (c) difficult situation

_____ (d) to force to do something because the law, one's conscience, etc. demands it

_____ (e) marked by no special feelings for or against something

_____ (f) excessive pride in one's looks or accomplishments

_____ (g) adopted; took on

_____ (h) overhasty, reckless

_____ (i) cut short

_____ (j) reverence; admiration; wonder

(2) Write a paragraph using three of the words from the list above. Use a separate piece of paper.

WRITING ABOUT IT

Use a separate piece of paper.

19

(1) Describe how values, attitudes, and customs have changed since 1868 when Louisa May Alcott wrote *Little Women*.

(2) The author uses dialogue to tell her story. Use dialogue to describe a sacrifice someone made for a person they love.

AN INCREDIBLE RECORD

ABOUT THE PASSAGE   No one had ever won more than five gold medals in a single Olympic Game, but in 1972 a young American changed all this with a remarkable display of athletic **prowess.** This is his story.

REASON FOR READING   Notice the method that this writer uses to present her information. Is it entirely chronological?

READ THE PASSAGE

It was the beginning of the 1972 Olympic Games. Mark Spitz, together with 12,000 other athletes from 124 nations, stood watching the opening **rites.** As the Olympic flame, relayed from Greece by almost 6,000 runners, was borne onto the field, Mark Spitz, like the other competitors, wondered what the next few days would bring.

Not only would he represent his country in seven different events, but he was expected to win them all! Could he do the impossible? Never in Olympic history had one athlete won more than five gold medals in a single year, and this year the competition was tougher than ever.

In addition, the last time Mark was **touted** to sweep the Olympics, he failed. At Mexico City in 1968, he had been entered in six races; then only a gawky, green, and somewhat cocky teenager, he had openly boasted, "Sure, I can win all six." But he managed to capture only two gold medals, and those were in relay events. In terms of the standards that he had set for himself, it was a **dismal** performance.

Mark, now twenty-two, had come a long way since then. The swimmer who stood in Munich's new domed stadium was still self-assured, but this time he seemed to show a quiet, mature confidence. His fellow athletes viewed him with respect instead of with jealousy and **disdain.** As he waited, what were his thoughts? He thought back upon those interminable hours spent in training and splashing his way to victory after victory, and of the people who had helped him become the champion that he was.

Of course, Mark's biggest influences were his parents. When Mark was only two, they lived in Hawaii and took him to the beach every day. Later, when they moved to Sacramento, California, they enrolled him in the swimming program at the local YMCA so that he would have the opportunity to develop his technique, and to test his skill against other youngsters.

"Swimming isn't everything," his father used to say. "Winning is." So when a rival team finally succeeded in outswimming his son, Mr. Spitz decided to send Mark to work with the coach whose students had beaten him.

Under Sherman Chavoor of the Arden Hills swim club, Mark was soon surpassing even his father's dreams of success. At ten, he set his first U.S. record by swimming the junior fifty-yard butterfly in thirty-one seconds. Chavoor, kindly and knowledgeable, has remained Mark's **mentor** to this day. He was the one who selected Mark's next coach, George Haines, when the family moved again.

Haines had already trained some extraordinary swimmers at the Santa Clara swim club, including Olympic winner Don Schollander, who won four gold medals at Tokyo in 1964. Mark rose at 5 a.m. daily to be at Santa Clara for the 6:30 practices, and his dedication paid off. He proved a match even for Schollander. In 1967, he broke five U.S. and three world records, won five gold medals at the Pan-American Games, and was named Swimmer of the Year by *Swimming World* magazine. No wonder he and his fans predicted he would win six medals in the 1968 Olympics!

Many factors probably contributed to that Mexico City disaster—overconfidence, the rivalry and ill-feelings that sprang up between Mark and his teammates, the tremendous pressure from the expectations of his parents, coach, and fans across the country, and, of course, the unnerving challenge of facing his first Olympics. Mark emerged from those Games hurt and overwhelmed by a feeling of defeat.

At that point, however, another coach came into his life to help set him on an **even keel** again. Jim ("Doc") Councilman of Indiana University not only improved Mark's skill but also taught him to put swimming in its proper **perspective.** He made sure that Mark got along well with his teammates and helped him to develop confidence in himself, with less of the show and **brashness** of earlier days. By the time of his college gradua-tion, Mark had accumulated three dozen new records, and he would go to Munich a new man, in complete command not only of his sport, but also of himself.

In the week that followed, he would win five events, tying the record of the Italian fencer, Nedo Nadi, in 1920. Then, as he faced his last two races, not only the Munich spectators, but the whole world—watching via television satellite—would be rooting for him. In all, he would set seven new records and become the first athlete to stand on the victor's platform seven times in one Olympic Games.

Not long before the Games, Mark said to reporters, "I want to swim at Munich and then quit. I never swam for glory, only for the satisfac-tion of being recognized as the best in the world." He achieved that goal.

THINKING IT OVER

(1) How does the author present information? Is it entirely chronological?

_____

(2) Mark Spitz's experience illustrates some of the problems a champion athlete must overcome. List three of them.

(a) _____

(b) _____

(c) _____

STUDYING THE PASSAGE

(1) Find the Main Idea: Choose one answer.
  (a) How a swimmer trains for the Olympics.
  (b) Why Mark Spitz decided to become a swimmer.
  (c) How Mark Spitz became an Olympic champion.
  (d) Why Spitz decided to quit swimming.   _____

(2) Find the Facts: Mark each one *true* or *false*.
  (a) Until 1972, no Olympic athlete had won more than five gold medals in one year.   (a) _____
  (b) Mark Spitz won all of his races in the Mexico City Olympics.   (b) _____
  (c) Mark has always been well liked by other athletes.   (c) _____
  (d) Mark did his first racing at the YMCA in Sacramento.   (d) _____
  (e) Mark Spitz said that good sportsmanship was the most important thing
      an athlete could learn.   (e) _____
  (f) Mark was Swimmer of the Year in 1967.   (f) _____

(g) Coach Jim Councilman saw to it that Mark got along well with his teammates. (g) _____

(h) Mark quit college in order to devote more time to his swimming. (h) _____

(3) Find the Order: Number the following in the order in which they appear in the passage.

(a) Mark set his first U.S. record when he was ten years old. (a) _____

(b) Can he do the impossible? (b) _____

(c) The whole world was watching via television satellite. (c) _____

(d) The Olympic flame is carried onto the field to open the 1972 Games. (d) _____

(e) Another coach came into his life to set him on an even keel. (e) _____

(f) Of course, Mark's biggest influences were his parents. (f) _____

(g) Mark would rise daily at 5 a.m. to get to Santa Clara for 6:30 practices. (g) _____

(h) At Mexico City in 1968, he and his fans had boasted that he would win six medals. (h) _____

(4) Go beyond the Facts: Which conclusion is *not* based on the passage?

(a) Mark's father gave him the driving desire to win.

(b) An arrogant attitude can be a handicap.

(c) George Haines did little to help Spitz.

(d) Jim Councilman was probably the most effective of Spitz's coaches. _____

(5) Determine the Writer's Style and Technique: Choose one answer.

(a) She appeals to the reader's senses.

(b) She uses a series of events to make a point.

(c) She personalizes the story by telling her own experiences.

(d) She relates the story to the reader's own life. _____

USING THE WORDS

(1) Words and Their Meanings: Find the boldfaced word for these definitions. One word has *two* meanings.

_____ (a) scorn; a feeling of contempt for what appears to be unworthy

_____ (b) ceremonies, rituals

_____ (c) the way something looks from a given point according to its size, shape, or distance.

_____ (d) impudence, forwardness, sauciness

_____ (e) a faithful adviser

_____ (f) (from horseracing slang) praised highly; publicized as being of great worth

_____ (g) disastrous, dreadful; showing or causing gloom

_____ (h) sense of proportion; true relation of objects or events to one another in terms of importance or value

_____ (i) in an even, steady way; stable (from part of a boat that keeps it from toppling over)

_____ (j) extraordinary ability, skill

(2) Write a paragraph using three words from the list above. Use a separate piece of paper.

WRITING ABOUT IT

Use a separate piece of paper.

(1) Find out about another sports figure who has been successful and write a short biography about his or her life. When writing about someone's life, you don't have to relate the events in the order in which they occurred. Sometimes an account is more interesting if you start with a major event in the person's career, as the writer does in this passage.

(2) What do you think are the attributes of a champion?

JOAN OF ARC

ABOUT THE PASSAGE   Can you imagine a seventeen year old girl leading an army into battle? That is what Joan of Arc did in France's Hundred Years' War against the British. She won the battle, but later came to a terrible end. Do you know what happened to her?

REASON FOR READING   To learn about an extraordinary historical figure.

READ THE PASSAGE

The city of Rouen in northern France possesses a simple statue of a young girl. It calls to mind an awesome story—one of strength and dedication to an ideal, and of cruelty, jealousy, and persecution. The flames of prayer candles now play shadows on the statue of a girl for whom flames once burned to ashes. This young woman inspired and led her nation with courage, honesty, and energy as she fought to **liberate** France from the English during the Hundred Years' War.

Joan was a hard-working, religious child who tended her father's cattle in Domrémy, France. At the age of thirteen, she believed that she had heard the voice of God. Later, she claimed that she had visions and had communicated with St. Michael, St. Catherine, and St. Margaret. She announced that her mission was to lay **siege** to Orléans, a city then held by the English. Because the French were desperate, they finally decided to make use of seventeen-year-old Joan.

Under her direction, the French armies were victorious at Orléans and in several other important battles. The **heir** to the throne, Charles VII, was at last crowned King of France. France was filled with wild enthusiasm. Joan believed that her **divine** mission had been accomplished with the coronation of Charles, but he pressed her into further service. She began to lose battles and was captured by the Burgundians (French who were allies of the English) and handed over to the enemy.

Joan was honored, respected, and helped by Charles VII and his generals only as long as she was successful and useful to them. In addition, there was another factor working against Joan at this time. Apparently the English and some of the French were dismayed that a teenager, and especially a young woman, had been successful where thousands of older, well-trained, well-educated men had failed. At this point, the University of Paris, acting in English interests, urged that Joan be turned over to the Church. Soon she was in the hands of the Burgundian bishop, Pierre Cauchon.

Joan was brought to court to be tried on matters of faith and morals. Her **interrogators** accused her of crimes against God and the Church, and tried to persuade her to confess. They tried to obtain information from her about Charles VII, to whom she always remained loyal. They criticized her attitude and behavior. The church charged her with claiming to have divine **revelations**, making prophecies, signing her letters "Jesus" and "Mary," wearing men's clothing, and claiming that her saints spoke to her in French and not in English. They also tried to embarrass her with ridiculous questions. For example, they wanted to know whether St. Michael had long hair or not. She answered cleverly by asking why it should have been cut off. They tried to trap her into admitting that she had not obeyed Church law, but Joan maintained that she had always done what God had dictated. Of the seventy charges, all but twelve were dropped. Joan would not give a false confession, and she declared that if she were tortured, she would at a later time deny any confession given under torture.

The court found Joan guilty of witchcraft and **heresy** and handed her over to the English **secular** power. On May 30, 1431, Joan of Arc was burned to death at the stake. Charles VII, the king for whom Joan had worked and fought, made no attempt to save her. Twenty-five years too late, her trial was declared unjust. Five hundred years later, in 1920, she was declared a saint.

Unquestionably, Joan was as feared as she was **revered.** The same strength, honesty, and courage that made the people of France adopt her as their symbol of hope, also brought fear to the people around her who were in positions of authority.

At the time of her execution, Joan of Arc was nineteen years old.

THINKING IT OVER

(1) Why did the French decide to make use of Joan? _____

_____

(2) Name two important things she managed to do for France:

    (a) _____

    (b) _____

(3) How did she die? _____

STUDYING THE PASSAGE

(1) Find the Main Idea: Choose one answer.
    (a) Joan of Arc was a young troublemaker.
    (b) Joan of Arc was such a strong and effective person that it was not until after her death that her strength could be officially admitted.
    (c) King Charles VII of France was a weak man.
    (d) Joan was foolish to take so many risks.   _____

(2) Find the Facts: Mark each one *true* or *false*.
    (a) Joan of Arc was made a saint almost five hundred years after she had died.   (a) _____
    (b) England and France were involved in what was called the Hundred Years' War.   (b) _____
    (c) King Charles VII tried to help Joan when she needed him most.   (c) _____
    (d) Joan was tried by the British Parliament in a fair trial.   (d) _____
    (e) Joan of Arc was an extraordinary young woman.   (e) _____
    (f) Joan of Arc was a young woman who tried to live by the word of God, as she saw it.   (f) _____
    (g) Joan was charged with trying to overthrow the government of France.   (g) _____
    (h) Bishop Cauchon was Joan's friend.   (h) _____

(3) Find the Order: Number the following in the order in which they appear in the passage.
    (a) At the time of her execution, Joan of Arc was nineteen years old.   (a) _____
    (b) Joan was a hard-working, religious child who tended her father's cattle.   (b) _____
    (c) The flames of prayer candles now play shadows on the statue of a girl for whom flames once burned to ashes.   (c) _____
    (d) As long as she was useful to the king and his generals, she was honored and respected.   (d) _____
    (e) At the age of thirteen, she believed she had heard the voice of God.   (e) _____

(f) French armies, under Joan's direction, won several important battles.   (f) _____

(g) The court found Joan guilty of witchcraft and heresy.   (g) _____

(h) Joan would not give a false confession.   (h) _____

(4) Go beyond the Facts: Choose one answer.
    (a) If Joan had not claimed to have divine guidance, the generals probably would never have permitted her to lead the army.
    (b) If Joan of Arc lived today, she would undoubtedly be hired by our present administration to try to solve some of our long-standing national problems.
    (c) Joan of Arc has been an enduring symbol of right and might conquering wrong for over five hundred years.
    (d) If Joan had only been imprisoned for life and not burned at the stake, she would not have been declared a saint.   _____

(5) Determine the Writer's Style and Technique: Choose one answer.
    (a) Uses facts to show cause and effect.
    (b) Uses a story to create an example of interpretation.
    (c) Uses a fable to make a moral point.
    (d) Uses an historical event to demonstrate that people in positions of authority often make mistakes.   _____

USING THE WORDS

(1) Words and Their Meanings: Find the boldfaced word for these definitions.

_____ (a) respected greatly, worshipped

_____ (b) belief in an opinion contrary to the teachings of the church

_____ (c) to free, as from oppression or bondage

_____ (d) a military blockade of a city or fort to force it to surrender

_____ (e) of or pertaining to the worldly rather than the spiritual

_____ (f) relating to or proceeding directly from a god

_____ (g) those who examine by formal questioning

_____ (h) one who is entitled to inherit property or position

_____ (i) things that are disclosed or made known

(2) Write a paragraph using three words from the list above. Use a separate piece of paper.

WRITING ABOUT IT

Use a separate piece of paper.

(1) Working in a group, or with the help of your teacher, write a trial scene for a play based on Joan of Arc's trial. Have the interrogators cross-examine Joan, and give her responses.

(2) Joan of Arc accepted a challenge—based on a message she thought came from God. Write about someone you know, or have read about, who rose to a challenge. Explain what the challenge was and how he or she met it.

THE BIGGEST CARRIER OF INFORMATION

ABOUT THE PASSAGE   Which is the biggest carrier of information?

(a) the telephone   (c) television
(b) radio   (d) none of these

REASON FOR READING   Read it as fast as you can and see how many details you can remember. Then, without rereading the passage or looking at the questions on the passage, answer the first writing question, which is: Write all you can remember about the biggest carrier of information. Then answer the questions.

READ THE PASSAGE

We send information from the East Coast to the West Coast, from our country to other countries, and even from the earth to satellites. We send it by telephone, radio, television, computer, and fax but the **volume** of information is increasing so rapidly that we urgently need new carriers to handle it.

In 1960, scientists discovered a new and fantastic carrier that could handle all the combined messages formerly **transmitted** by telephone, radio, and television. Known as the laser, it is an extremely narrow beam of light—the sharpest, purest, and most intense light ever seen.

Laser's are different from ordinary light. Ordinary light consists of waves that are called "incoherent light." This means the waves are of different frequencies; they are all jumbled together and the waves of light fly off in every direction. The light waves produced by the laser are "coherent." This means the waves are parallel and of the same size and **frequency,** each wave of light fitting closely with the one next to it. It is because the waves travel long distances without **scattering** that the laser has many uses in long distance communication.

Laser light has supershort wavelengths. Whereas radio waves, for example, are measured in meters, and television waves are measured in inches, the laser waves are measured in ten-millionths of an inch. Because the shorter the wavelengths are, the greater the amount of information that can be carried, lasers can be used to transmit great volumes of messages.

The laser has many uses in addition to transmitting information, and currently scientists are discovering still more. One of its most remarkable uses is in performing bloodless surgery. Its beam is so strong that it can painlessly burn away **warts** and wrinkles, and seal blood vessels with its great heat. Eye doctors use it to weld **detached** retinas into place and to remove cataracts, thus preventing loss of vision, as well as restore 20/20 vision to some people who are nearsighted. Dentists can use lasers to drill teeth painlessly.

The laser can also be used to cut very hard materials, such as diamonds; to light the ocean; and to study air pollution. It has enabled scientists to measure the distance from the earth to the moon to within fifteen feet of accuracy. It has even helped art dealers to **detect** art **frauds.**

Few realized, when the laser was first discovered, that it would provide us with so many benefits. Every day, it seems, new ways of using the laser are being discovered.

THINKING IT OVER

(1) What is the biggest carrier of information? _____

_____

(2) List three of its other uses:

    (a) _____

    (b) _____

    (c) _____

(3) What does *coherent* mean in this passage? _____

_____

STUDYING THE PASSAGE

(1) Find the Main Idea: Choose one answer.
    (a) Lasers are the best carrier of information.
    (b) We can use lasers to communicate with other planets.
    (c) Lasers are a new discovery that brings many benefits to humanity.
    (d) Lasers will make life more fun. _____

(2) Find the Facts: Mark each one *true* or *false*.
    (a) The laser beam was discovered in 1970. (a) _____
    (b) Laser's are different from ordinary light. (b) _____
    (c) The light waves produced by a laser are all of the same frequency. (c) _____
    (d) The light waves produced by a laser scatter in all directions. (d) _____
    (e) The laser light has very short wavelengths. (e) _____
    (f) Lasers can be used to perform bloodless surgery. (f) _____
    (g) Lasers can be used to cut hard materials. (g) _____
    (h) Scientists will probably discover more uses for the laser. (h) _____

(3) Find the Order: Number the following in the order in which they appear in the passage.
    (a) Laser waves are measured in ten-millionths of an inch. (a) _____
    (b) Ordinary light consists of waves that are called "incoherent light." (b) _____
    (c) It has even helped art dealers detect art frauds. (c) _____
    (d) The laser is an extremely narrow, sharp, pure, and intense beam of light. (d) _____
    (e) The shorter the wavelength, the greater the amount of information that can
        be carried. (e) _____
    (f) The laser has many uses in addition to transmitting information. (f) _____
    (g) The volume of information is increasing so rapidly we urgently need new
        carriers to handle it. (g) _____
    (h) The light waves produced by the laser are "coherent." (h) _____

(4) Go beyond the Facts: Which *one* of the following would probably *not* be a use for the laser?
    (a) Finding out about life in the deep waters of the sea.
    (b) Converting sea water into drinking water.
    (c) Helping to guide spaceships.
    (d) Removing a birthmark. _____

(5) Determine the Writer's Style and Technique: Which *one* method does the writer *not* use?

    (a) Includes definitions.

    (b) Makes a comparison.

    (c) Gives examples.

    (d) Gives quotes from scientific journals.   _____

USING THE WORDS

(1) Words and Their Meanings: Find the boldfaced word for these definitions. One word has *two* meanings.

_____   (a) quantity

_____   (b) the number of times any action or occurrence is repeated in a given period

_____   (c) disconnected

_____   (d) going apart in different directions

_____   (e) carried, conveyed, conducted

_____   (f) fakes, deceptions

_____   (g) discover

_____   (h) growths on the skin caused by a virus

_____   (i) degree of loudness of sounds

(2) Write a paragraph using three of the words from the list above. Use a separate piece of paper.

WRITING ABOUT IT

Use a separate piece of paper.

(1) Write all you can remember about the biggest carrier of information. Then check your account with the passage to see how much you remembered.

(2) The discovery of the laser has been one of the most important technological advances in our time. Find out more about the laser and its uses, and write a comprehensive report summarizing your research.

Selection 10—Subject: Science
Theme: The World around Us

NATURE'S MISCHIEF MAKES MIRAGES*

ABOUT THE PASSAGE   We all know **mirages** are not real. Or do we? Read this passage and see if it changes your mind.

REASON FOR READING   To help you understand a scientific explanation of a mysterious, natural phenomenon.

READ THE PASSAGE

Putting on a **sorcerer**'s hat, nature poises its magic wand over a desert wasteland, and suddenly the horseman at our right appears to be riding in a lake. Then, just as abruptly as the water appeared, it vanishes into thin air, leaving only parched sand. Nature has just performed one of its most amazing sleight-of-hand tricks—a mirage.

Through the ages mirages have **baffled** people. A team of American naturalists, for example, trekked miles over Arctic wastes to explore an island that they saw in the distance. But when the sun went down, so did the "magnificent peaks."

Nature's practical joke can sometimes turn into a disastrous **deception.** Wreck-strewn beaches tell of ships led to destruction by **phantom** lighthouses. Mountain slopes hide the twisted bodies of airplanes as a result of pilots' swerving to miss imaginary peaks only to crash into real ones.

Mirages were often labeled **hallucinations** or miracles, but mirages are real. In 1798, a French scientist named Gaspard Monge provided an explanation for their occurrence.

Put a pencil in a glass half-filled with water. Notice that the submerged end of the pencil seems separated from the half above the water. The distorted image is created by light waves passing through the water. Because water **density** differs from air density, it bends the light waves, causing the underwater image of the pencil to shift. The result is an optical **illusion** that makes the pencil look broken.

A similar thing happens in the atmosphere to create a mirage. When cool and warm air layers overlap, the difference in their density bends the light waves passing through the two layers.

In summer, motorists experience a simple mirage when the road ahead seems to disappear into a pool of water. The "lake" appears when light rays streak downward through a heavier, cool air layer and hit a lighter, warmer layer just above the pavement. What the driver thinks is water is actually a patch of reflected sky, shimmering above the sun-heated asphalt.

The reverse can happen when a warm air layer hangs over a cooler layer. Images of earthbound objects are projected into the sky.

The higher the air layers the more mysterious the illusion. Like mirrors in a carnival fun house, the lens-like layers can turn images upside down and even reflect them across great distances.

In 1941, startled passengers aboard a Norwegian train saw a tropical island, complete with lagoon and battleship, floating in the sky outside their car window.

In the Strait of Messina, between Italy and Sicily, ideal weather conditions sometimes produce the famous *fata morgana* mirage, a **turreted** city rising in the sky.

Nature's mischief with light confuses wildlife as well as humans. At times, ducks swooping down for a swim find only a dust bath instead.

*From "Light Mischief Makes Mirages," *National Geographic School Bulletin,* vol. 46, no. 26, March 25, 1968. Reprinted by permission of the *National Geographic School Bulletin.*

THINKING IT OVER

(1) What are the dangers of mirages? _____

_____

(2) Who first came up with an explanation of mirages? _____

_____

_____

STUDYING THE PASSAGE

(1) Find the Main Idea: Choose one answer.
    (a) Nature—the practical joker.
    (b) How mirages cause disasters.
    (c) What causes mirages.
    (d) How to bend a pencil.   _____

(2) Find the Facts: Mark each one *true* or *false*.
    (a) Mirages have baffled people until the last few centuries.   (a) _____
    (b) A French scientist gave a scientific explanation for mirages.   (b) _____
    (c) Science has proven that mirages don't exist.   (c) _____
    (d) Water density differs from air density.   (d) _____
    (e) The density of cool air is the same as that of warm air.   (e) _____
    (f) The pool of water you see when driving along the road on a hot day
       is a reflection of the sky.   (f) _____
    (g) Mirages can be seen in the sky as well as on land.   (g) _____
    (h) The higher the warm air layers, the more mysterious the illusion.   (h) _____

(3) Find the Order: Number the following in the order in which they appear in the passage.
    (a) Mirages can be upside-down reflections of objects.   (a) _____
    (b) Motorists experience a simple mirage when the road ahead seems
       to disappear into a pool of water.   (b) _____
    (c) Nature's practical joke can turn into a disastrous deception.   (c) _____
    (d) Norwegians saw a tropical island from their train window.   (d) _____
    (e) Put a pencil in a glass half-filled with water.   (e) _____
    (f) Italians sometimes see a turreted city rising in the sky.   (f) _____
    (g) Putting on a sorcerer's hat, nature poises its magic wand over a desert wasteland.   (g) _____
    (h) In 1798 Gaspard Monge supplied an explanation of mirages.   (h) _____

(4) Go beyond the Facts: What is the effect of the last two sentences?
    (a) They leave you feeling that animals are stupid and comical.
    (b) They leave you feeling that people are just animals after all.
    (c) They make you understand that different kinds of creatures can have the
       same kind of experience.
    (d) They make you feel thirsty.   _____

(5) Determine the Writer's Style and Technique: Which *one* does the writer *not* use?

    (a) Examples and anecdotes.

    (b) Analogy.

    (c) Scientific explanation.

    (d) Dialogue.   _____

USING THE WORDS

(1) Words and Their Meanings: Find the boldfaced word for these definitions. *Three* words fit the first definition.

   _____   (a) something that appears to exist in a certain place but that, in fact, does not

   _____   (b) ghostly; visible to the eye but not really existing

   _____   (c) frustrated, perplexed

   _____   (d) a trick; something misleading

   _____   (e) a magician

   _____   (f) the quantity of something per unit of volume or area

   _____   (g) furnished with ornamental structures in the form of towers

(2) Write a paragraph using three of the words from the list above. Use a separate piece of paper.

WRITING ABOUT IT

Use a separate piece of paper.

(1) Without going back over the passage, explain how a mirage is created. Describe a simple experiment that proves this, and give examples of mirages.

(2) As mirages show, things are not always what they seem. Describe some incidences you have come across that show this to be true, and explain the consequences. If you have a hard time coming up with incidences, make up some likely ones, such as: a product that doesn't turn out to be as it is advertised; someone who is friendly, but is saying things behind people's backs; etc.

THE STRUGGLE FOR SURVIVAL

ABOUT THE PASSAGE   A famous scientist, Charles Darwin (1809–1882), once wrote about the "struggle for survival." Do you know what he meant by this?

REASON FOR READING   To learn about a scientific **concept** through descriptive writing.

READ THE PASSAGE

He glided through the dark shadows, aware of every movement, every change in the forest. His body was black, sleek, and muscular, broken only by a few battle scars; his eyes were yellow and **wary.** Padded feet hiding sharp claws carried him silently on his daily search for food. Stopping every few yards to sniff the breeze, his head erect, his torn ears turning nervously, he was a beautiful sight. He was like a miniature panther. He represented the magnificence of the **feline** world, the **cunning** of a practiced hunter.

Reclining motionless atop a convenient rock with the stage of nature's drama below, I was afforded an excellent view of this animal. He stopped and looked around and tested the air warily, but did not notice me. In the grass, which formed a velvet carpet for nature's stage, there was a quick motion. He tensed and pounced all in one swiftly calculated movement. The discovery that his victim was only a scaly lizard caused him disdainfully to let it go. What a prey for one such as he! After all, he was a hunter. The tiny lizard gained freedom and found a **haven** under the rock on which I lay.

The cat sat proudly on his haunches and licked the paw that had stopped the lizard for that moment, as if to wash away even the slightest memory of such **degradation.** He glanced around—perhaps to see if anyone had witnessed his embarrassment—and satisfied that he had not been observed, lowered his body into the depths of a shadow where, resting his head on his forepaws, he awaited further signs of life.

A cautious quiet pervaded the secluded **glen.** I waited impatiently. The chief actor in the scene was my symbol of prowess in the hunting world. Suddenly, I heard the flutter and clatter of several nervous birds in the treetops. I was not the only one who noticed these new actors invading the scene. He stiffened on his haunches and assumed a ready pose. I could almost see his whiskers twitching with excitement. He watched the warm, feathered tidbits with more than a simple, interested curiosity. It was plain that there was careful plotting going on behind that hungry stare.

The sunlight filtering through the treetops focused on a cluster of these birds who were pecking nervously in the grass. He lurked nearer the edge of the shadows and watched every bird intently until one perky sparrow grew brave enough to hazard a flight to the edge of the clearing. Suddenly the black image pounced. A last struggle amid flying feathers, and a piercing chirp marked the end of the sparrow's life. The triumphant hunter carried his victim over the dewy grass and faded into the shadows. I stared at the few deserted feathers scattered near the edge of the clearing. How quickly the life of that innocent victim had been extinguished. And yet its death meant life for another.

In this natural setting, my old feline friend had taken on a new character of cunning and magnificence; he seemed so much more **alien** to me surrounded by the trees and shadows than dozing lazily by the crackling fire with his body quiet, his long tail curled companionably around his nose, and his eyes so softly yellow. And yet I understood his need to return to nature, to test his hunting prowess, and to take his place in the endless drama of nature.

THINKING IT OVER

(1) What is the "struggle for survival"? _____

(2) Who won the struggle in this passage? _____

STUDYING THE PASSAGE

(1) Find the Main Idea: Choose one answer.
    (a) Cats eat birds.
    (b) There is both tragedy and beauty in nature's struggle.
    (c) Cats don't like lizards.
    (d) Cats change character when they sit by the fire.   _____

(2) Find the Facts: Mark each one *true* or *false*.
    (a) The cat had torn ears.   (a) _____
    (b) The cat was grey.   (b) _____
    (c) The cat had yellow eyes.   (c) _____
    (d) The cat let the lizard go.   (d) _____
    (e) The cat hid on a rock.   (e) _____
    (f) Two birds came into the glen.   (f) _____
    (g) The cat belonged to the author.   (g) _____
    (h) The wild setting made the author see her cat in a new way.   (h) _____

(3) Find the Order: Number the following in the order in which they appear in the passage.
    (a) The cat pounces on a lizard.   (a) _____
    (b) Birds flutter into the glen.   (b) _____
    (c) The author lies silently on a rock.   (c) _____
    (d) The author describes her cat at home.   (d) _____
    (e) The cat licks its paw.   (e) _____
    (f) The cat pounces on a sparrow.   (f) _____
    (g) The cat glides through the forest toward the glen.   (g) _____
    (h) The lizard slithers under a rock.   (h) _____

(4) Go beyond the Facts: Choose one answer.
    (a) Cats will always be winners.
    (b) In nature the strongest usually survive.
    (c) Birds are relatively unintelligent.
    (d) The smallest animals usually die.   _____

(5) Determine the Writer's Style and Technique: Choose one answer.
    (a) She describes.
    (b) She compares.
    (c) She shows cause and effect.
    (d) She lists facts.   _____

USING THE WORDS

(1) Words and Their Meanings: Find the boldfaced word for these definitions. One word has *two* meanings.

_____   (a) careful, watchful

_____   (b) belonging to another person or place; strange, foreign

_____   (c) skillful in cheating or tricking; crafty

_____   (d) idea

_____   (e) hidden seclusion, a place of safety

_____   (f) lowering of grade, rank, or status

_____   (g) a secluded, narrow valley

_____   (h) a stranger; a foreign-born resident who is not a naturalized citizen of his or her new country

_____   (i) of or relating to cats or the cat family

(2) Write a paragraph using three of the words from the list above. Use a separate piece of paper.

WRITING ABOUT IT

Use a separate piece of paper.

(1) Give another example which illustrates the struggle for survival. Try to make your description as interesting, colorful and imaginative as possible. Before you start, reread the passage, paying special attention to Darwin's choice of words. Notice how specific and effective they are. Decide on your "hunter" and "victim," then write down all the words you can think of to describe them. Use a thesaurus to find words you have not used before. Select the words you think will best describe the hunter and victim, then write your account of their meeting.

(2) Humans, of course, are part of the evolutionary chain in the struggle for survival. We eat meat, fish, eggs, etc. However, some people contend that we should not kill and eat other living things. Do you agree with this? Give reasons for your answer.

LIFE'S MYSTERY

ABOUT THE PASSAGE   The gift of life is an unfathomable mystery. This selection tells you how water may have been one of life's original sources.

REASON FOR READING   As with any scientific data, you should read this selection carefully, trying to remember and relate all the facts. Notice the use of such words as: "contend," "assume," and "theorize."

READ THE PASSAGE

As the morning rays of the sun danced upon the waters of the lake, a small band of wild elephants played lazily along the shallow edge of the cool water. Suddenly, from the hidden recesses of a rock high up on a cliff, a rifle shot cracked through the crisp morning air and found its mark. As panic struck, the herd pounded for cover, seeking shelter in the dense forest nearby. Near the prone body of the dying elephant, the blue water took on the unfamiliar hue of red.

Both life and death are unfathomable mysteries. How is it that at one moment sparkling life can be locked into a princely elephant and in another instant be extinguished? And where did that vital, mysterious spark come from originally?

Currently, some scientists contend that the very water into which the elephant's lifeblood was flowing is connected to one of life's original sources. Working on the research of a Russian biochemist named A. I. Oparin, they assume that the **primitive** atmosphere, quite different from our own, contained methane, ammonia, carbon dioxide, water vapor, helium, and hydrogen. Scientists suggest that the twin energy sources of the sun and lightning promoted a chemical combination, causing atoms to form new molecules and compounds. Over billions of years innumerable "chance combinations" occurred and accumulated in the **primeval** waters of the young earth. Slow evolution produced clusters of molecular substances, and eventually there emerged some type of primitive cell.

It is in this cell, this microscopic unit of matter, that scientists today theorize that the secret of life is contained. The electron microscope has revealed within the cell the presence of intricate systems of membranes. Across these, dynamic forces operate to maintain a **homeostatic,** or balanced environment that permits the existence of life as we know it today. With the **vigilance** of a night watchman, the processes of **diffusion, osmosis,** and active transport **relentlessly** regulate the movement of materials in and out of the cell.

Today it is possible for a biochemist to analyze the cell down to the smallest atom of which it is composed. The most common elements found in both plant and animal cells are carbon, nitrogen, hydrogen, oxygen, phosphorus, sulfur, and several trace elements. Independently these substances are nonliving or "inorganic." However, when combined in the proper proportions, these lifeless substances become part of a living system. After much detective work on the part of researchers, evidence points to the fact that it is the **nucleus** of the cell, as the "command center" containing the vital DNA **chromosomal** material, that indirectly determines the biochemical activities and specific characteristics of all cellular organisms.

Could these cells, which give life to plants and animals alike, really have originated from the earth's primeval waters? Science is full of unanswered questions, and scientists will go on pursuing the mysteries of life.

37

THINKING IT OVER

(1) Some scientists theorize that water holds the secret to the beginning of life. According to these scientists, what part did water play in the evolution of the cell?_____

_____

_____

(2) What is the significance of words such as *contend, assume,* and *theorize*?

_____

_____

STUDYING THE PASSAGE

(1) Find the Main Idea: Choose one answer.
   (a) The origin of living cells.
   (b) An unfathomable mystery.
   (c) How a cell functions.
   (d) The uncertainty of science.   _____

(2) Find the Facts: Mark each one *true* or *false*.
   (a) The sun and lightning provided energy to form new molecules.   (a) _____
   (b) Scientists who analyze cells are called nuclear physicists.   (b) _____
   (c) Billions of years may have passed before some primitive type of cell emerged. (c) _____
   (d) Osmosis, diffusion, and active transport regulate the flow of materials
       into and out of cells.   (d) _____
   (e) Two elephants lay dead on the shore.   (e) _____
   (f) Carbon and nitrogen are two of the most common ingredients
       of plant and animal cells.   (f) _____
   (g) Intricate systems of membranes contain the vital DNA
       chromosomal material.   (g) _____
   (h) The earth's early atmosphere was different from our present day atmosphere. (h) _____

(3) Find the Order: Number the following in the order in which they appear in the passage.
   (a) Combined in proper proportion these lifeless substances become
       part of a living system.   (a) _____
   (b) Science is full of unanswered questions.   (b) _____
   (c) Today it is possible to analyze a cell down to its smallest atom.   (c) _____
   (d) Intricate systems of membranes have been detected with the electron microscope. (d) _____
   (e) Eventually there emerged some type of primitive cell.   (e) _____
   (f) Suddenly a rifle shot cracked through the morning air.   (f) _____
   (g) Slow evolution produced clusters of molecular substances.   (g) _____
   (h) Over the years, innumerable "chance combinations" occurred and
       accumulated in the primeval waters.   (h) _____

(4) Go beyond the Facts: From the passage, what *one* thing can be concluded about the author?
   (a) She agrees with the theories described.
   (b) She is not a religious person.

(c) She disagrees with the theories described.

(d) She thinks that the theories might be correct but does not regard them as proven beyond a doubt. _____

(5) Determine the Writer's Style and Technique: Choose one answer.

(a) Uses precise definitions to explain what something is.

(b) Presents both sides of an argument.

(c) Gives a detailed, logical argument supported with facts.

(d) Summarizes a theory. _____

USING THE WORDS

(1) Words and Their Meanings: Find the boldfaced word for these definitions. One word has *two* meanings.

_____ (a) watchfulness

_____ (b) central part; core

_____ (c) crude, simple, unsophisticated

_____ (d) of or concerning the earliest or original stage of something

_____ (e) balanced

_____ (f) steadily and persistently

_____ (g) of or concerning the thread-like chains of genes that control and transmit hereditary characteristics

_____ (h) the gradual passage of liquid through a membrane barrier until its molecules are evenly concentrated on both sides of the membrane

_____ (i) the process of becoming spread out or dispersed

_____ (j) of or relating to the earliest ages

(2) Write a paragraph using three of the words from the list above. Use a separate piece of paper.

WRITING ABOUT IT

Use a separate piece of paper.

(1) Make up a test of ten questions on the passage. Then exchange your test with that of a classmate and see if you can answer each other's questions.

(2) Water plays a vital role in our lives, apart from giving us life itself. Write an essay on "Water in Our Lives," describing the many different ways we need, use, and enjoy water, as well as the dangers and destruction it can bring. Write down all your ideas. Then be sure to make a clear outline, zeroing in on the key aspects you want to write about.

WHERE'S THE MATTER?*

ABOUT THE PASSAGE   Explorers of the sky have been receiving signals that indicate that up to 90% of the universe is unable to be seen and that an incredible new type of object exists in space.

REASON FOR READING   This is a difficult passage. Read it carefully to grasp its main ideas. Then try to put the main ideas into your own words.

READ THE PASSAGE

The mysterious signals come from the deep **recesses** of space, traveling at the speed of light. High above the earth a tiny orbiting satellite, called Explorer 42, picks them up and relays them to a ground station. Their final destination is a space agency computer in Greenbelt, Maryland.

The computer tells researchers that the signals are coming from an object in our **galaxy** that is many thousands of billions of miles from earth. At first the researchers blinked in amazement at what they had discovered.

They learned that the object seems to have a diameter smaller than that of earth, yet the energy it produces makes it 1,000 times more powerful than the sun. Even more startling, the object doubles its energy output within a tenth of a second and just as suddenly reduces it again. That's like the sun suddenly doubling in brightness, and then quickly returning to its normal self.

When originally discovered, this strange object, now named Cygnus X-1, bewildered scientists with its power. "We have a completely new physical object that requires a solution," said the physicist Herbert Gurksy. The most recent theory is that Cygnus X-1 is a time tunnel or black hole in space.

The possibility of black holes has caught the fancy of scientists since it was first **propounded** in the 1930s, but the signals from Cygnus X-1 mark the first time a black hole has actually been detected.

Today the Hubble Space Telescope, orbiting 370 miles above our atmosphere, has not only confirmed the existence of black holes, it offers some unobstructed views of the universe—pictures of stars exploding and colliding galaxies.

The idea of black holes is based on the widely held theory that the galaxies are flying apart at a gradually decreasing rate. The theory contends that this braking effect must be caused by **gravitational** force from matter, such as other galaxies. However, there is not enough visible matter to exert such a tremendous force. The proposed explanation is that the missing matter exists in the form of black holes.

At first glance, a theory of a hole in space where time stands still—so that a fraction of a second becomes eternity, and where all things simply disappear from sight would seem to belong to the realm of science fiction. Yet, to astronomers, it is far from fantasy.

The astronomers believe Cygnus X-1 may illustrate what happens when very large stars "die." All stars eventually change in nature. The **thermonuclear** fires that power them die out, and they begin to squeeze themselves ever-smaller with their own gravitational pressure. The result varies according to the size of the star, which may have two to five times the mass of the sun. It is believed that this squeezing continues until its atoms crush together with such force, that only the nuclei remain. It becomes a neutron star—virtually a

*From "Where's the Matter" by David Brand, *The Wall Street Journal,* vol. CLXXIX, no. 118. Adapted by permission of *The Wall Street Journal.*

huge atomic nucleus ten miles across, on which a tablespoon of sand would weigh 40,000 billion tons.

Scientists believe that this pattern of "death" can be taken one stage further by revealing many stars whose masses are more than five times that of the sun. Scientists believe that since the gravitational force would be so much greater, it is logical to theorize that the star would squeeze itself into a ball of matter so dense and so small, it would simply disappear. It would, in fact, become a black hole in space.

As a massive star begins to shrink, its gravitational field remains just as powerful because there is still the same amount of matter. However, because the matter has been so **condensed**, the gravitational field becomes more and more intensely focused. By the time the star has been squeezed to a certain point, called its "gravitational radius," the force of gravity has become so extreme, that not even light can escape. There is only blackness. At this point, an odd thing happens. The star turns itself inside out, like a glove, and everything becomes reversed.

Thus, gravity instead of being a pulling force, becomes a force that pushes. This push of gravity creates a tunnel in space, a black hole. (This pushing-type of gravity affects only matter drawn into the black hole. Once outside, the hole exerts the normal pulling-type gravity—thus the hole pulls matter in and then pushes it forever through the tunnel in space.)

Even more curiously, time and space also become reversed inside the tunnel. According to the theory, distance becomes a time-like measurement, always moving forward and never being able to stand still or go back. Time becomes a space–like measurement, not moving forward but standing still.

Remo Ruffini, a physicist at Princeton University, has imagined the shattering effect on the occupants of a spaceship that entered a black hole and then somehow escaped from the push of gravity. Since time in the tunnel would stand still, he says, it would seem to the space travelers that only a flash of a second had passed, but in the world of time outside, perhaps billions of years would have elapsed.

In actuality, says Ruffini, nothing could escape from a black hole. Once inside one, an object **literally** disappears. What happens to it? Ruffini theorizes that inside the hole an object loses its separate identity as it is stripped down to its atoms by the tidal forces created by the push of gravity.

THINKING IT OVER

(1) Many scientists believe that the galaxies are speeding away from each other, growing farther apart in space.

   (a) What is happening to the rate at which the galaxies are flying apart? _____

   _____

   _____

   (b) What does the theory state is the cause of such a change? _____

   _____

   _____

   (c) What problem seemed to contradict the theory, and how did the idea of black holes in space help to solve it? _____

   _____

   _____

STUDYING THE PASSAGE

(1) Find the Main Idea: Choose one answer.
    (a) The whole universe may eventually cease to exist.
    (b) Scientists are constantly making new discoveries.
    (c) Black holes may explain some changes in the nature of stars and the universe.
    (d) All stars, sooner or later, disintegrate.   _____

(2) Find the Facts: Mark each one *true* or *false*.
    (a) Black holes have been confirmed by the Hubble Space Telescope.   (a) _____
    (b) When the thermonuclear fires that power them burn out, stars begin
        to grow larger.   (b) _____
    (c) Cygnus X-1 seems to be smaller than the earth.   (c) _____
    (d) The theory of black holes originated in the 1930s.   (d) _____
    (e) As a massive star shrinks, so does its gravitational field.   (e) _____
    (f) To astronauts in a black hole, billions of years would seem like
        a flash of a second.   (f) _____
    (g) A neutron star's atoms are so closely packed together that only
        their nuclei remain.   (g) _____
    (h) A black hole's gravity is so strong that even light is pulled toward
        it and cannot escape.   (h) _____

(3) Find the Order: Number the following in the order in which they appear in the passage.
    (a) The star would squeeze itself into a ball of matter so dense and so
        small it would simply disappear.   (a) _____
    (b) Time becomes space-like, not moving forward, but standing still.   (b) _____
    (c) Researchers blinked in amazement at what they had discovered.   (c) _____
    (d) An object loses its separate identity.   (d) _____
    (e) Signals from Cygnus X-1 mark the first time a black hole has actually
        been detected.   (e) _____
    (f) Cygnus X-1 may show what happens when very large stars "die."   (f) _____
    (g) The hole pulls matter in and then pushes it forever through the tunnel in space.   (g) _____
    (h) Distance becomes time-like, always moving forward.   (h) _____

(4) Go beyond the Facts: Which one is not true?
    (a) Black holes are "black" because no light escapes from their vicinity
        to reach our eyes.
    (b) The way in which Cygnus X-1 produces signals is not described
        in the passage.
    (c) Black holes are invisible and consist of nothing.
    (d) Distance in a black hole is like time on earth, because an object entering
        the hole can move in only one direction, and it will never stop moving.   _____

(5) Determine the Writer's Style and Technique: What kind of newspaper piece is this?
    (a) A straight news report.
    (b) An editorial.
    (c) A feature story providing information in an interesting way.
    (d) A report for astronomers only.   _____

USING THE WORDS

(1) Words and Their Meanings: Find the boldfaced word for these definitions. One word has *two* meanings.

_____ (a) pertaining to the natural forces of attraction between bodies of matter

_____ (b) offered for discussion or consideration

_____ (c) made more compact; reduced in extent

_____ (d) actually; in fact

_____ (e) pertaining to the high-temperature fusion of atoms, as in the hydrogen bomb or the sun

_____ (f) a huge system or grouping of stars, dust, and gases, such as the Milky Way

_____ (g) short rest periods

_____ (h) remote or hidden places

(2) Write a paragraph using three of the words from the list above. Use a separate piece of paper.

WRITING ABOUT IT

Use a separate piece of paper.

(1) Read the passage again, underlining or highlighting the key facts. Try to explain in your own words what the writer is telling you. It will help to compare your answers to "Thinking It Over."

(2) Write a science fiction story that begins with the first two sentences of this passage.

SYMBOLIC LOGIC

ABOUT THE PASSAGE   The following problem is given again at the end of this passage. Compare the answer you give now to the answer you give after reading the selection.

Hypothesis: Premise 1 — All sardines are fish.
Premise 2 — All fish can swim.

Conclusion: All _____

REASON FOR READING   To see if you can follow the explanation in order to solve a particular type of problem.

READ THE PASSAGE

Suppose we want to express the idea that all dogs are animals. If we let D represent the set of all dogs and A represent the set that contains all animals, then set A contains set D; that is, set D is a proper subset of A. We can illustrate this concept by using a Venn diagram. In the Venn diagram below, we have drawn a smaller circle to represent D, the set of dogs, inside the larger circle A, the set of all animals. The diagram shows that every dog is an animal.

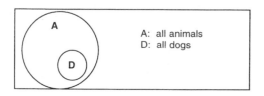

We could also divide the set D into three subsets: the set of big dogs, the set of medium dogs, and the set of small dogs. We would then **modify** our diagram to include this information (See Diagram 2).

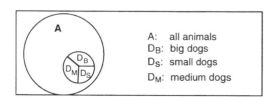

The way the smaller circle is subdivided to include the whole area of D indicates not only that all dogs are animals, but that there is no dog that is not a big dog, a medium dog, or a small dog.

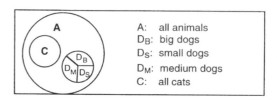

To our previous example we have added set C, the set of all cats (See Diagram 3). The nonoverlapping circles C and D illustrate the fact that although all cats are animals and all dogs are animals, no cat is a dog and vice versa.

Sets C and D are examples of **disjointed** sets because they have no elements in common. In Venn diagrams, such sets are represented by two nonoverlapping circles or closed areas. Such illustrations represent the idea of "no" or "none" in symbolic logic.

Venn diagrams can also be used to represent the concept of "some." Diagram 3 shows that the set of animals includes animals that are cats and animals that are not cats (for instance, dogs). Therefore, the diagram illustrates the premise that some animals are cats and some aren't. It is important to note that in mathematical logic, the term *some* means one or more, and hence, could conceivably mean *all*. So we could conclude that *some* cats are animals, although it's more precise to state that *all* cats are animals.

Making conclusions with Venn diagrams is an example of **deduction,** or deductive reasoning, a process in which conclusions and new knowledge are deduced from certain given statements or premises. Venn diagrams can be very valuable aids in this type of reasoning, for a single picture is often simpler and clearer than a verbal explanation. These diagrams in no way constitute a formal proof, nor are they satisfactory when solving complicated problems, but they do give us valuable insights into the deductive process. Consider the following deductive **arguments:**

Hypothesis:

Premise 1—All dogs are mammals.

Premise 2—All mammals are animals.

Conclusion: All dogs are animals.

The Venn diagram that illustrates this argument is:

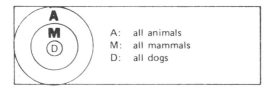

Since the circle representing dogs is entirely within the circle representing mammals, the first premise is illustrated. The same is true for the second premise since the circle that represents mammals is entirely within the circle that represents animals. The conclusion can be determined from the diagram. Notice that it is impossible to draw the diagram so that it correctly illustrates the two premises without also correctly illustrating the given conclusion. In other words, the conclusion is **inescapable**.

If the premises of an argument do not lead to a valid conclusion, a different situation arises in constructing a Venn diagram. For example, consider the following argument:

Hypothesis:

Premise 1—No teachers are students.

Premise 2—All students are clever.

Conclusion: No teacher is clever.

Leaving aside any **misgivings** about the truth of the premises or the conclusion, deductively this is not a **valid** conclusion. We get an indication of this when we try to draw a Venn diagram. There are three different ways we can represent the premises; one indicates the given conclusion, and the others do not.

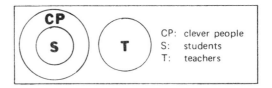

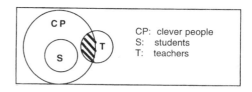

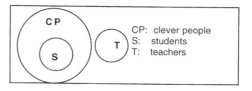

According to the premises, the only requirement is that the circles representing teachers and students be disjointed, and that the circle representing students be entirely within the circle representing clever people. Hence, all three diagrams correctly represent the premises of the argument, but they lead to different conclusions. The fact that the premises can be represented with multiple diagrams indicates that there isn't *one*, valid conclusion. Therefore, the argument is invalid because it suggests that there is only one conclusion.

In summary, Venn diagrams are helpful in solving simple cases of deductive reasoning. Closed areas or circles can represent the premises of the argument and the logical relationships of "all," "some," or "none" between them. Once all of the premises have been illustrated with a Venn diagram, the diagram can be used to determine whether a conclusion is valid.

THINKING IT OVER

(1) What is the correct conclusion to the argument given in About the Passage? _____

_____

(2) What is the use of a Venn diagram? _____

_____

STUDYING THE PASSAGE

(1) Find the Main Idea: Choose one answer.
   (a) No cat is also a dog.
   (b) Diagrams can help to settle arguments.
   (c) All premises do not necessarily lead to valid conclusions.
   (d) Venn diagrams can be used to illustrate logical relationships.   _____

(2) Find the Facts: Mark each one *true* or *false*.
   (a) D is the set that contains all the dogs.   (a) _____
   (b) The set of all dogs is a subset of the set of all animals   (b) _____
   (c) In mathematical logic, "all" means "at least one."   (c) _____
   (d) Circles that partially overlap are used to show disjointed sets.   (d) _____
   (e) Venn diagrams show the exact number of items in each set.   (e) _____
   (f) An invalid argument leads to a single inescapable conclusion.   (f) _____
   (g) In deductive reasoning, conclusions and new knowledge are derived
       from given premises.   (g) _____
   (h) Venn diagrams can show whether a conclusion is valid.   (h) _____

(3) Find the Order: Number the following in the order in which they appear in the passage.
   (a) The conclusion is inescapable.   (a) _____
   (b) Set D is a proper subset of A.   (b) _____
   (c) Both diagrams fit the premises correctly, but they lead to three different conclusions. (c) _____
   (d) Nonoverlapping circles illustrate the relationship "no" or "none."   (d) _____
   (e) No cat is a dog and vice versa.   (e) _____
   (f) A single picture is simpler and clearer than a verbal explanation.   (f) _____
   (g) The area belonging to both circles at the same time indicates "some."   (g) _____
   (h) The way circle D is subdivided shows that there is no dog that is not big,
       medium or little.   (h) _____

(4) Go beyond the Facts: Choose two answers.
   (a) A Venn diagram can help to show whether a given premise is in fact true.
   (b) A conclusion may be logically valid yet not a true statement of fact if the
       premises contain false statements.
   (c) Deductive reasoning is the best method for discovering new knowledge.
   (d) Premises that are factually correct do not necessarily lead to a logically
       valid conclusion.   _____   _____

(5) Determine the Writer's Style and Technique: Choose one answer.
   (a) Builds to a conclusion that is revealed in the end.
   (b) Begins with a brief summary of points to be covered.
   (c) Proceeds from simple examples to more complex ones.
   (d) Introduces a complex problem, then breaks it down into simple steps. _____

USING THE WORDS

(1) Words and Their Meanings: Find the boldfaced word for these definitions. One word has *two* meanings.

_____ (a) a dispute, a quarrel

_____ (b) sound, logically correct

_____ (c) to make a small or partial change

_____ (d) having no elements in common

_____ (e) doubts, suspicions

_____ (f) assumption; proposition set forth as the basis for reasoning

_____ (g) a statement or belief that is taken for granted and used as the basis for a theory

_____ (h) a course of reasoning aimed at proving some point

_____ (i) impossible to escape or avoid; inevitable

_____ (j) the act of deriving a logical conclusion from statements or beliefs that are taken for granted

(2) Write a paragraph using three of the words from the list above. Use a separate piece of paper.

WRITING ABOUT IT

Use a separate piece of paper.

(1) Draw Venn diagrams that illustrate the following: all sardines are fish; some sardines are fish; no sardines are fish—the relationship, "some"; and the relationship, "none."

(2) As you read previously, Venn diagrams are one method of illustrating the concept of "some." Make up your own illustration demonstrating the concept of "some," and draw a Venn diagram depicting this.

A PROBLEM IN LOGIC

ABOUT THE PASSAGE   There was a bank robbery. Who was the thief—Sylvie, Elizabeth, Romana, or Ellen?

REASON FOR READING   To follow the steps involved in solving a logical reasoning problem.

READ THE PASSAGE

1) Sylvie and Elizabeth were in the bank when the bank robber walked in.
2) Both Ramona and the bank teller had gone to the same high school with the physician.
3) The bank teller, who recognized Ellen, was planning to attend the same concert that Sylvie was to attend.
4) Sylvie did not know Elizabeth.
5) All the people who attended high school together knew each other.
6) One of these women was a computer **programmer.**

Who is the bank teller, the bank robber, the computer programmer, and the physician?

To solve this problem we will have to make some deductions from the information given in the six statements. Let's use a chart to record our reasoning and fill it in step-by-step.

	Bank Teller	Bank Robber	Computer Programmer	Physician
Sylvie				
Elizabeth				
Ramona				
Ellen				

From statement 1, we can conclude that neither Sylvie nor Elizabeth is the bank robber since they were in the bank when the robber walked in. So we put 0s in the bank robber column opposite Sylvie and Elizabeth's names.

From statement 2, we can conclude that Ramona is not the bank teller, nor is she the physician. We put 0s for her in the **appropriate** boxes. So our chart looks like this:

	Bank Teller	Bank Robber	Computer Programmer	Physician
Sylvie		O		
Elizabeth		O		
Ramona	O			O
Ellen				

Now, from statement 3, we can deduce that neither Sylvie nor Ellen is the bank teller; therefore, Elizabeth is the bank teller, so we put a X in the appropriate square. If Elizabeth is the bank teller, she cannot be the computer programmer or the physician; again we put 0s in the appropriate boxes. Now our chart looks like this:

	Bank Teller	Bank Robber	Computer Programmer	Physician
Sylvie	O	O		
Elizabeth	X	O	O	O
Ramona	O			O
Ellen	O			

From statements 2, 4, 5, and 6, we can deduce that Sylvie is not the physician because she does not know Elizabeth (the bank teller). So Sylvie must be the computer programmer. We put a X and 0s in the correct boxes. Now we can see that the physician must be Ellen, and Ramona must be the bank robber. Our chart supports our reasoning:

	Bank Teller	Bank Robber	Computer Programmer	Physician
Sylvie	O	O	X	O
Elizabeth	X	O	O	O
Ramona	O	X	O	O
Ellen	O	O	O	X

The kind of reasoning used to solve this problem is called "deductive reasoning." It is the same kind of logic implicit in the Venn diagram approach of Selection 14. Deductive reasoning usually involves moving from certain general statements or premises to new conclusions and new knowledge about a specific situation. In our case, we moved step-by-step from six general statements to the specific knowledge of the robber's identity.

Another type of reasoning is **induction,** or inductive reasoning. The inductive process consists of moving from the specific to the general. For example, when an apple fell on Isaac Newton's head, he added this specific **instance** to the many other times he had observed falling objects, and reached the general conclusion we know today as the law of gravity.

One important point to note about inductive reasoning is that Newton or, for that matter, anyone could not have observed *every* time an object fell to the ground, so a conclusion arrived at by inductive reasoning is never one-hundred percent certain.

Today, when scientists use **formulas** to solve problems, they rely on inductive reasoning, while detectives hot on the trail of Ramona-the-bank-robber would be more likely to use deductive reasoning.

THINKING IT OVER

(1) Who was the thief? _____

(2) What is inductive reasoning? _____

_____

STUDYING THE PASSAGE

(1) Find the Main Idea: Choose one answer.
    (a) Solving a mystery with brilliant deductions.
    (b) Two methods of logical reasoning and how they differ.
    (c) The impossibility of being absolutely certain.
    (d) Charts as aids to reasoning.   _____

(2) Find the Facts: Mark each one *true* or *false*.
    (a) Elizabeth is the computer programmer.   (a) _____
    (b) Sylvie did not attend high school with the other three women.   (b) _____
    (c) Deductive reasoning moves step-by-step from general statements
        to a conclusion.   (c) _____
    (d) Sylvie knows Ramona.   (d) _____
    (e) The inductive reasoning process moves from general to specific.   (e) _____
    (f) Deductive reasoning is implicit in the logic used for Venn diagrams.   (f) _____
    (g) Observing a number of known instances of some event is part of the
        deductive process.   (g) _____
    (h) A conclusion drawn by inductive reasoning is never one-hundred percent certain.   (h) _____

(3) Find the Order: Number the following in the order in which they appear in the passage.

    (a) When we move from general statements to new conclusions, we are using deductive reasoning.   (a) ____

    (b) When scientists use formulas to solve problems, they rely on inductive reasoning.   (b) ____

    (c) Inductive reasoning moves from the specific to the general.   (c) ____

    (d) One of these women is a computer programmer.   (d) ____

    (e) There is no one left to be the physician except Ellen.   (e) ____

    (f) A detective hot on the trail of Ramona-the-bank-robber would be more likely to use deductive reasoning.   (f) ____

    (g) We conclude that neither Sylvie nor Elizabeth can be the robber.   (g) ____

    (h) Newton reached a general conclusion that lead to the law of gravity.   (h) ____

(4) Go beyond the Facts: Which *one* of the following assumptions or "rules of the game" is *not* required in order to solve the bank robbery problem?

    (a) There is only one bank robber.

    (b) All of the women mentioned are actually in the bank at the time of the theft.

    (c) Each woman has only one role in the problem; no one can have one of the jobs mentioned and be the bank robber as well.

    (d) The robber must be someone mentioned in the six premises.   ____

(5) Determine the Writer's Style and Technique: Which *one* of the following is *not* used by the author to make the passage clear?

    (a) Clear topic sentences.

    (b) Simple sentence structure.

    (c) Metaphor and analogy.

    (d) Step-by-step organization.   ____

USING THE WORDS

(1) Words and Their Meanings: Find the boldfaced word for these definitions.

_____   (a) the act of coming to a general conclusion after studying particular facts

_____   (b) a group of symbols and figures showing the elements in a chemical compound

_____   (c) a person that works out a series of operations to be performed by a mechanism

_____   (d) an example; something that shows or proves; an occasion or case

_____   (e) just right for the purpose, suitable

(2) Write a paragraph using three of the words from the list above. Use a separate piece of paper.

WRITING ABOUT IT

Use a separate piece of paper.

(1) Explain the difference between "deductive" and "inductive" reasoning.

(2) Solve the following problem, using a chart to record your reasoning. Mrs. Cunningham says the house has to be cleaned. She tells her five children that each one must clean a room. The rooms that need to be cleaned are: the living room, the den, the kitchen, the bathroom, and the playroom. Which room does each child clean?

    (a) Stephanie refuses to clean sinks.
    (b) Ray hates putting the toys away in the toy box.
    (c) Stan and Charles always fluff up the cushions on the couches when they clean.
    (d) You can enter the den through the kitchen, but the living room is on the other side of the house.
    (e) There are no couches in the kitchen, bathroom, or playroom.
    (f) Charles and Bruce enjoy talking to each other as they work.
    (g) The toy box is in the playroom.

TWO PASSAGES FROM THE BIBLE

ABOUT THE PASSAGES   The Bible outsells all other books written in English. Its **profound** thoughts have affected people for hundreds of generations. The King James translation (A.D. 1611) used in this passage is regarded as one of the most outstanding literary achievements in our language.

REASON FOR READING   Notice that the straightforward phrases and sentences create an overall tone of dignified simplicity, while the use of questions and answers and repeated ideas gives rise to the rhythmical cadence of poetry.

What is the simple message conveyed by both of these passages? Are they relevant to our society?

READ THE PASSAGES

THE GOOD SAMARITAN

25   And, behold, a certain lawyer stood up, and tempted him, saying, Master, what shall I do to inherit eternal life?

26   He said unto him, What is written in the law? how readest though?

27   And he answering said, Thou shalt love the Lord my God with all thy heart, and with all thy soul, and with all thy strength, and with all thy mind; and thy neighbor as thyself.

28   And he said unto him, Thou hast answered right: this do, and thou shalt live.

29   But he, willing to justify himself, said unto Jesus, And who is thy neighbor?

30   And Jesus answering said, A certain man went down from Jerusalem to Jericho, and fell among thieves, which stripped him of his **raiment,** and wounded him, and departed, leaving him half dead.

31   And by chance there came down a certain priest that way: and when he saw him, he passed by on the other side.

32   And likewise a Levite,[1] when he was at the place, came and looked on him, and passed by on the other side.

33   But a certain Samaritan,[2] as he journeyed, came where he was: and when he saw him, he had **compassion** on him,

34   And went to him, and bound up his wounds, pouring in oil and wine, and set him on his own beast, and brought him to an inn, and took care of him.

35   And on the morrow when he departed, he took out two pence, and gave them to the host, and said unto him, Take care of him; and whatsoever thou spendest more, when I come again, I will repay thee.

36   Which now of these three, thinkest thou, was neighbor unto him that fell among the thieves?

37   And he said, He that showed mercy on him. Then said Jesus unto him, Go, and do thou likewise.

Luke 10:25-37

---

1. A member of the tribe of Levi, from which assistants to the Jewish priests were chosen.

2. A man from Samaria, a region of Israel that lay to the north of Jerusalem. Levites and Samaritans were traditionally hostile to one another.

CHARITY

1 Though I speak with the tongues of men and of angels, and have not charity, I am become as sounding brass, or a tinkling **cymbal.**

2 And though I have the gift of prophecy, and understand all mysteries, and all knowledge; and though I have all faith, so that I could remove mountains, and have not charity, I am nothing.

3 And though I **bestow** all my goods to feed the poor, and though I give my body to be burned, and have not charity, it profiteth me nothing.

4 Charity suffereth long, and is kind; charity envieth not; charity **vaunteth** not itself, is not puffed up,

5 Doth not behave itself **unseemly,** seeketh not her own, is not easily provoked, thinketh no evil;

6 Rejoiceth not in **iniquity,** but rejoiceth in the truth;

7 Beareth all things, believeth all things, hopeth all things, endureth all things.

8 Charity never faileth: but whether there be prophecies, they shall fail; whether there be tongues, they shall cease; whether there be knowledge, it shall vanish away.

9 For we know in part, and we prophesy in part.

10 But when that which is perfect is come, then that which is in part shall be done away.

11 When I was a child, I spake as a child, I understood as a child, I thought as a child: but when I became a man, I put away childish things.

12 For now we see through a glass, darkly; but then face to face: now I know in part; but then shall I know even as also I am known.

13 And now **abideth** faith, hope, charity, these three; but the greatest of these is charity.

I Corinthians 13: 1-13

THINKING IT OVER

(1) What is the simple message conveyed by both passages? _____

_____

(2) "The Good Samaritan" is an example of a parable. What is a parable? _____

_____

(3) We use the term "a good samaritan" today. What does it mean? _____

_____

(4) Explain what the writer of "Charity" means in verses 11 and 12. _____

_____

(5) The King James translation was adapted in 1611. More recent Bible translators use "love" for the word "charity" in I Corinthians because over the centuries our word "charity" has changed its meaning. What parts of the passage seem to support the newer version?

_____

_____

STUDYING THE PASSAGE

(1) Find the Main Idea: Which statement do *both* passages suggest?
   (a) Charity begins at home.
   (b) You should always help people in distress.
   (c) Charity is superior to all other human qualities.
   (d) If you are not charitable to others you will not receive charity in return.   _____

(2) Find the Facts: Mark each one *true* or *false*.
   (a) "Levite" means someone who helps other people.   (a) _____
   (b) The man was going from Jericho to Jerusalem.   (b) _____
   (c) The priest passed by the other side.   (c) _____
   (d) The Samaritan later fell among thieves.   (d) _____
   (e) If one has the gift of prophecy, one can understand all mysteries.   (e) _____
   (f) Charity suffereth long and is kind.   (f) _____
   (g) One should not rejoice in iniquity, but in truth.   (g) _____
   (h) When that which is perfect appears, then that which is in part (imperfect)
       shall be done away with.   (h) _____

(3) Find the Order: Number the following in the order in which they appear in the passage.
   (a) They departed and left him half dead.   (a) _____
   (b) He brought him to an inn and took care of him.   (b) _____
   (c) And he answering said, Thou shalt love the Lord thy God with all thy heart.   (c) _____
   (d) And he said, He that showed mercy on him.   (d) _____
   (e) And he said unto him, Thou hast answered right: this do, and thou shalt live.   (e) _____
   (f) A certain priest came along that way.   (f) _____
   (g) But he said unto Jesus, And who is my neighbor?   (g) _____
   (h) And when he saw him, he had compassion on him.   (h) _____

(4) Go beyond the Facts: Choose two answers.
   (a) Both passages suggest that we must demonstrate charity by observable acts.
   (b) Both passages suggest that charity is more than observable acts.
   (c) The first passage suggests that charity should be demonstrated by observable
       acts, while the second passage suggests that one can act "charitably" and
       still not be charitable.
   (d) The first passage suggests charity is a matter of giving to others; the second
       passage suggests that charity is something that is within us.   _____   _____

(5) Determine the Writer's Style and Technique: Choose one answer.
   (a) Both passages use repetition to reinforce ideas.
   (b) Both passages contain imagery and figurative language.
   (c) Both passages use simple narrative.
   (d) Both passages personalize their message.   _____

USING THE WORDS

(1) Words and Their Meanings: Find the boldfaced word for these definitions.

_____ (a) having intellectual depth and insight

_____ (b) wickedness; gross injustice

_____ (c) sympathetic awareness of another's distress and desire to lessen it

_____ (d) A concave brass plate that produces a loud, clashing tone when struck

_____ (e) garments, attire

_____ (f) to present as a gift; to give

_____ (g) not in accordance with established standards; unsuitable for the time or place

_____ (h) boasts, makes a vain display of one's own worth

_____ (i) remains, continues

(2) Write a paragraph using three of the words from the list above. Use a separate piece of paper.

WRITING ABOUT IT

Use a separate piece of paper.

(1) Write your own parable called "The Good Samaritan."

(2) Write a song, poem or lyrical prose (writing with rhyme and repetition) on love of humanity vs. romantic love.

Selection 17—Subject: Philosophy, Logic, and Math
Theme: How about That?

ANCIENT NUMERICAL CONCEPTS*

ABOUT THE PASSAGE   This passage explains how a man from ancient Greece and his followers, connected numbers with ideas.

REASON FOR READING   To notice how facts need to be presented clearly and logically in a mathematical selection, such as this one.

READ THE PASSAGE

Numbers played a very important part in the life of the ancient Greeks, particularly in the life of a man called Pythagoras. He and his followers thought that everything in the world was made of numbers. They maintained that the **ultimate** number was ten, which they called the "holy tetractys." In her book, *A New Mathematics Reader,* Evelyn Sharp explains that the Greeks picked ten because $1 + 2 + 3 + 4 = 10$. Specifically, the tetractys was represented by this triangular arrangement of ten dots, showing that ten is composed of rows of 1, 2, 3, and 4.

To the Greeks, the first four counting numbers had a special meaning; they associated them with the four elements—fire, water, air, and earth. Their sum, therefore, encompassed all of the elements of life and stood for the ideal.

So persistent were they in this belief, that they thought the whole universe must **embody** this principle. As a result, they believed that there must be ten heavenly bodies—although they could find only nine. So they invented another one, which they named the counterearth and figured that it was always in the wrong part of the sky to be seen.

Their picture of the universe was of a central fire, or guiding force, around which revolved ten moving bodies. From the center outward, these were the counterearth, the earth, moon, sun, the five planets known at the time (Mercury, Venus, Mars, Jupiter, Saturn), and lastly the stars, which they thought were all fixed to a single sphere and therefore counted as one.

This concept was advanced for the time and is closer to the truth than the ancient and medieval idea of the earth standing still, with all the stars and planets in the solar system revolving around it.

The Greeks identified numbers with human **characteristics**, including gender. The odd numbers were thought to be masculine, good, and celestial—the even numbers were feminine, evil, and earthly. There was a **correspondence** here with Chinese numerical concepts in which the odd numbers were considered bright, male, and **beneficent**, and the even numbers dark, female, and **malevolent**. (Note: women were not highly regarded by the ancients.)

In addition, individual numbers had their own distinguishing traits. *One* stood for reason, and was not considered a true number, but rather as the source from which all the numbers were generated by adding ones together. It was not classified as either even or odd.

Two represented opinion, which can be **wavering** or indecisive. We sometimes say, for example, "I'm of two minds about is matter."

Four was associated with justice because it is the product of equals, that is, two times two. We still use "square" with this meaning as shown in

*From *A New Mathematics Reader* by Evelyn Sharp. Copyright 1967, 1966, 1964 by Evelyn Sharp. Reprinted by permission of E. P. Dutton and Company, Inc.

the expressions, "a square deal," "fair and square," "a square shooter."

Five was the marriage number, made from the union of two, the first even (feminine) number, and three, the first odd (masculine) number.

Seven was a virgin number because of the first ten counting numbers, it alone is neither a **factor** nor a product.

Numerology was very important to the ancient Greeks, as reflected in Pythagorean philosophy.

THINKING IT OVER

(1) Why did Pythagoras and his followers pick ten as the ultimate number? _____

_____

(2) Which numbers had a special meaning to the ancient Greeks and stood for the ideal? What did they

represent? _____

_____

STUDYING THE PASSAGE

(1) Find the Main Idea: Choose one answer.
    (a) The first four counting numbers encompassed everything and stood for the ideal.
    (b) The significance of numbers for Pythagoras and the ancient Greeks.
    (c) Fire is the guiding force.
    (d) Individual numbers had their own distinguishing characteristics. _____

(2) Find the Facts: Mark each one *true* or *false*.
    (a) The Greeks thought that there must be ten heavenly bodies. (a) _____
    (b) The Greeks thought that the earth moved about the sun. (b) _____
    (c) The odd numbers were considered feminine. (c) _____
    (d) Feminine numbers were considered evil and earthly. (d) _____
    (e) The number ten was the holy tetramorph. (e) _____
    (f) Five was the marriage number. (f) _____
    (g) Women are more malevolent than men. (g) _____
    (h) The Chinese, as well as the Greeks, identified numbers with human characteristics. (h) _____

(3) Find the Order: Number the following in the order in which they appear in the passage.
    (a) The heavenly bodies revolved around a central fire. (a) _____
    (b) The whole universe must embody the ideal number ten. (b) _____
    (c) Odd numbers were thought to be masculine. (c) _____
    (d) Four was identified with justice. (d) _____
    (e) They invented another planet and named it the counterearth. (e) _____
    (f) Even numbers were thought to be feminine. (f) _____
    (g) There must be ten heavenly bodies. (g) _____
    (h) They identified the numbers with human characteristics. (h) _____

(4) Go beyond the Facts: Choose one answer.
   (a) Pythagoras developed basic mathematical and astronomical principles that we still use today.
   (b) The ancient Greeks believed in astrology.
   (c) The ancient Greeks knew that Uranus, Neptune, and Pluto existed.
   (d) The pyramids were built to symbolize the holy tetractys.   _____

(5) Determine the Writer's Style and Technique: Which *one* of the following best describes the way the writer presents facts?
   (a) She gives examples.
   (b) She makes comparisons.
   (c) She shows cause and effect.
   (d) She tells a story.   _____

USING THE WORDS

(1) Words and Their Meanings: Find the boldfaced word for these definitions.

   _____   (a) showing indecision, swaying to and fro

   _____   (b) doing or producing good

   _____   (c) extreme, utmost, basic, or elemental

   _____   (d) distinguishing traits

   _____   (e) an agreement or sameness; a match

   _____   (f) displaying evil or vicious ill will toward others

   _____   (g) any of two quantities that form a given product when multiplied together

   _____   (h) embrace, incorporate

(2) Write a paragraph using three of the words from the list above. Use a separate piece of paper.

WRITING ABOUT IT

Use a separate piece of paper.

(1) Make a chart showing what each number, 1 to 10, symbolized.

(2) The Greeks gave great importance to numbers. Describe what numbers mean to you. Do you have a favorite number? Do you think some numbers are lucky, and others unlucky? Do you associate different colors with numbers? Or, are numbers merely a page of math problems to be completed by tomorrow; the score of your last basketball game; or the price of a pizza?

HOW TO OUTWIT YOUR OPPONENT

ABOUT THE PASSAGE   When you play a game with someone, you naturally want to win. How you decide on the best way to win may be influenced by some very **innovative** thinking that has taken place in mathematics and philosophy during the twentieth century.

REASON FOR READING   To follow the logical explanation for the use of two game strategies.

READ THE PASSAGE

Uncertainty in life has always been something humans have had to contend with. Mathematicians have been interested in ways to make accurate **inferences**, to make estimations, and to test hypotheses accurately. Of all possible courses of action, which is best? During the twentieth century several theories were written about games and the nature of **strategy**.

Game theory is a branch of mathematics that studies strategy, whether in business, selling new products, war, or in games of competition and sport. It should not be confused with **probability** theory, which applies to situations where all events happen (or fail to happen) according to luck or chance. Strategy is controllable by the players; luck is not. Game theory helps one adopt the best variations in play to avoid being beaten.

When you and your opponent are locked in combat, what is the best strategy to follow? No matter what your **scheme**, there is always the

chance that your opponent will discover it and beat you. This is particularly true if the two of you are evenly matched.

To prevent your opponent from **thwarting** your plan, game theory holds that the only way to be sure your adversary is unaware of your plan of action is if you are unaware of it yourself. In other words you **randomize** your strategy by using some device of chance, such as drawing by lot or with a spinner. You create an unpredictable pattern for mixing your plays. For example, if you wanted to **bluff** 10 percent of the time, you could write *bluff* on one slip of paper and *don't bluff* on nine slips of paper. Then you would draw the slips of paper from a hat. Since you yourself do not know in advance whether you are going to bluff, how can your opponent possibly out-guess you?

Strategies may be either pure (simple) or mixed (randomized). A pure or simple strategy is an advanced list of instructions telling you exactly what to do in every possible circumstance according to the moves your opponent makes. Tic-Tac-Toe is a game in which pure strategy can be used. Complete information regarding the outcome is available for every possible move, by both you and your opponent. Thus, if the players are evenly matched, the game will always end in a tie; one can lose only by making a mistake.

But more often complete information is not possible, so on-the-spot decisions have to be made. This is when using a randomized or mixed strategy is beneficial.

THINKING IT OVER

(1) What is the difference between game theory and probability theory? _____

_____

_____

(2) According to the passage, what is the benefit of using a randomized strategy? _____

_____

STUDYING THE PASSAGE

(1) Find the Main Idea: Choose one answer.
  (a) Game theory should not be confused with probability theory.
  (b) Game theory explains how to use strategy.
  (c) Theory of games is an ancient way of dealing with uncertainty.
  (d) Game theory is a branch of mathematics. _____

(2) Find the Facts: Mark each one *true* or *false*.
  (a) Probability relies on strategy. (a) _____
  (b) Mathematicians have been interested in uncertainty. (b) _____
  (c) Game theory helps a player adopt the best variations in play to avoid being beaten. (c) _____
  (d) You must keep to a consistent pattern of plays in order to win. (d) _____
  (e) One way to randomize strategy is to use some device of chance, such as a spinner. (e) _____
  (f) Strategies are usually pure. (f) _____
  (g) A pure strategy is an advanced list of instructions covering all possible moves. (g) _____
  (h) In a mixed strategy, complete information is available on every possible move. (h) _____

(3) Find the Order: Number the following in the order in which they appear in the passage.
  (a) There is always a chance that your opponent will discover your strategy. (a) _____
  (b) Game theory helps make the best of a bad situation. (b) _____
  (c) Strategy is controllable by players; luck is not. (c) _____
  (d) Game theory is used in business and war. (d) _____
  (e) One can only lose by making a mistake. (e) _____
  (f) Tic-Tac-Toe is a game in which pure strategy can be used. (f) _____
  (g) A spinner can be used to make an unpredictable pattern for mixing your moves. (g) _____
  (h) To keep from being beaten, the best strategy is not to know your own strategy. (h) _____

(4) Go beyond the Facts: Which *two* statements seem the most logical extensions of the passage?
   (a) You could use game theory in chess or bridge, but not in dice or roulette.
   (b) Game theory is not applicable to business or politics.
   (c) Game theory is a mathematical model of real life situations.
   (d) Game theory does not apply to games that involve more than two players.   _____ _____

(5) Determine the Writer's Style and Technique: Which *one* of the following best describes the way the writer presents the facts?
   (a) Uses facts to explain an idea.
   (b) Makes an analogy to show what something is.
   (c) Tells a story to illustrate a fact.
   (d) Uses comparison and contrast to define something.   _____

USING THE WORDS

(1) Words and Their Meanings: Find the boldfaced word for these definitions.

   _____   (a) to fool another person by a false show of strength

   _____   (b) conclusions derived from facts or premises

   _____   (c) characterized by a new idea, method, or device

   _____   (d) likelihood of the occurrence of an event

   _____   (e) to arrange without any definite order

   _____   (f) a plan of action, sometimes unethical

   _____   (g) overall planning designed to gain some objective or to defeat an opponent

   _____   (h) blocking, frustrating, defeating

(2) Write a paragraph using three of the words from the list above. Use a separate piece of paper.

WRITING ABOUT IT

Use a separate piece of paper.

(1) Plan and write up a strategy. It can be a plan to outwit an opponent in a game, a plan to catch up on your backlog of homework or to tackle your next research report, or a plan to achieve a goal. Whatever you choose, it must require a well-thought-out plan with a series of specific steps that can be implemented.

(2) Try to outwit a classmate. Play a game of strategy (chess, tic-tac-toe, or another game) with a partner. During the first match, use a pure strategy; then use a random strategy during the second match. After the games, write up a conclusion, describing and explaining whether a pure strategy or a random strategy was more successful for you.

THE MYSTERY OF DEATH*

ABOUT THE PASSAGE   Life and death—these are the two things that have mystified humans throughout the ages. This tale gives an African perspective of the origin of death.

REASON FOR READING   To see how imagination as well as reason can provide answers to basic questions.

READ THE PASSAGE

Long, long ago there was a great **famine** in the world, and a certain young man, while wandering in search of food, strayed into a part of the **bush** where he had never been before. **Presently** he perceived a strange mass lying on the ground. He approached and saw that it was the body of a giant, whose hair resembled that of white men in that it was silky rather than woolly. It was of an incredible length, and stretched as far as from Kracho to Salaga. The young man was properly awed at the spectacle, and wished to withdraw, but the giant, noticing him, asked what he wanted.

The young man told about the famine and begged the giant to give him some food. The latter agreed on condition that the youth would serve him for a while. This matter having been arranged, the giant said that his name was Owuo, or Death, and he then gave the boy some meat.

Never before had the boy tasted such fine food, and he was well pleased with his bargain. He served his master for a long time and received plenty of meat, but one day he grew homesick, and he begged his master to give him a short holiday. The latter agreed, on the condition that the youth promise to bring another boy in his place. So the youth returned to his village and there persuaded his brother to go with him into the bush and serve Owuo in his **stead**.

Later the youth became hungry and returned to Owuo. He again ate all he wanted and worked for the master. But nowhere did he see his brother, who Owuo said was away on business.

The next time the youth grew homesick Owuo asked him to send as replacement a girl whom he could marry. The youth sent his sister with her slave girl to the giant.

Soon again the youth longed for the taste of meat, but this time when he returned to the bush the giant was not so friendly. Nevertheless, the giant allowed him to eat. To his horror the youth recognized the meat he was about to eat. It was the flesh of his sister and the slave girl.

Thoroughly frightened, he escaped and ran back to the village, where he told the elders what had happened. The alarm was sounded at once, and everyone went out to the bush. When they drew near the giant they grew afraid at the sight of so evil a monster.

They went back to the village and discussed what to do. At last it was agreed to go to Salaga, where the end of the giant's hair was, and set fire to it. After, this was done, and the hair was burning well, they returned to the bush and watched the giant. At last the fire reached his head, and in a moment the giant was dead.

The villagers approached him cautiously, and the young man noticed magic powder, which had been **concealed** in the roots of the giant's hair. No one could say what power this medicine might have, but an old man suggested that no harm

*Adapted from "The Origin of Death," in *African Folktales and Sculpture* (Bollingen Series XXXII), Copyright 1952, 1964 by the Bollingen Foundation, edited by Paul Radin and James Johnson Sweeney, and based on a story in A. W. Cardinall, *Tales Told in Togoland,* Oxford University Press, 1931.

would be done if they sprinkled some of it on the bones and meat in the hut. To the surprise of everyone, the girls and the boy at once returned to life.

The youth, who still had some of the powder left, **proposed** to put it on the giant. But that suggestion caused a great uproar; the people feared Owuo might come to life again. As a **compro-mise**, the boy sprinkled it into the eye of the dead giant. At once the eye opened and the people fled in terror.

Alas, it is from that eye that death comes. For every time Owuo shuts that eye, a person dies— and, unfortunately for us, he is forever blinking and winking.

THINKING IT OVER

(1) What explanation does the myth give for the fact that people die? _____

_____

_____

(2) Why did the myth have to end with Owuo forever blinking? _____

_____

(3) Why do you think the main person in the story is a youth?   _____

_____

STUDYING THE PASSAGE

(1) Find the Main Idea: Choose one answer.
   (a) People of all cultures wish to escape death.
   (b) Death is always a giant, sleeping in the African bush.
   (c) Famine brings death.
   (d) The boy shouldn't have experimented with the magic powder.   _____

(2) Find the Facts: Mark each one *true* or *false*.
   (a) This is a recent folk tale from Africa.   (a) _____
   (b) The giant's hair was incredibly long and silky.   (b) _____
   (c) The youth woke the giant up and asked him questions.   (c) _____
   (d) The young man was searching for a safe place in which to live.   (d) _____
   (e) In exchange for the meat the boy had to work for Owuo.   (e) _____
   (f) Each time the youth got homesick he sent one of his sisters to work for Owuo. (f) _____
   (g) The youth recognized his brother's body and realized that he was dead.   (g) _____
   (h) By using the magic powder, the people were able to kill Owuo.   (h) _____

(3) Find the Order: Number the following in the order in which they appear in the passage.
   (a) The giant asks the youth to send him a bride in exchange for a visit home.   (a) _____
   (b) The youth and giant make a bargain: food in exchange for work.   (b) _____
   (c) The youth discovered that Owuo had killed his sister and the slave girl.   (c) _____
   (d) The brother and two girls return to life.   (d) _____
   (e) The magic powder is sprinkled on the eye of the dead giant; it blinks.   (e) _____
   (f) A young man searching for food finds a giant instead.   (f) _____
   (g) The village elders learn about Owuo and his crimes.   (g) _____
   (h) The boy gets homesick and sends his brother as a substitute servant.   (h) _____

(4) Go beyond the Facts: After reading this passage, we can conclude which *one* of the following?
  (a) Magic never works.
  (b) There is no way to escape death.
  (c) Africa has never had periods of starvation.
  (d) Everyone gets homesick.   _____

(5) Determine the Writer's Style and Technique: Choose one answer.
  (a) Refers to scientific facts.
  (b) Presents an imaginative explanation for the facts of life.
  (c) Uses rhyming words.
  (d) Asks questions so that readers will decide for themselves. _____

USING THE WORDS

(1) Words and Their Meanings: Find the boldfaced word for these definitions.

_____   (a) a period of extreme hunger and starvation

_____   (b) uncleared or uncultivated country

_____   (c) hidden

_____   (d) the place of a person or thing as filled by a substitute

_____   (e) formed or put forward a plan or intention; set forth for acceptance
                                   or rejection

_____   (f) soon, before long

_____   (g) a settlement in which each side gives up some of its demands

(2) Write a paragraph using three of the words from the list above. Use a separate piece of paper.

WRITING ABOUT IT

Use a separate piece of paper.

(1) Write your own myth explaining death.

(2) Imagine a world without death. Would this be positive or negative?

OZYMANDIAS

ABOUT THE PASSAGE   Ozymandias is a broken statue located in the sands of Egypt; it is also the title of a poem about this statue.

REASON FOR READING   This poem, written by the English poet, Percy Bysshe Shelley,* makes important points about life, accomplishment, death, and time. Read to understand what these points are.

READ THE PASSAGE

1   I met a traveler from an **antique** land,
Who said—"Two vast and trunkless legs of stone
Stand on the desert . . . Near them, on the sand,
Half sunk, a **shattered visage** lies, whose frown,
5   And wrinkled lip, and **sneer** of cold command,
Tell that its **sculptor** well those passions read
Which yet **survive,** stamped on these lifeless things,`
The hand that **mocked** them, and the heart that fed,
And on the **pedestal,** these words appear:
10   My name is Ozymandias, King of Kings,
Look on my Works, ye Mighty, and despair!
Nothing beside remains. Round the decay
Of that colossal Wreck, boundless and bare
The lone and level sands stretch far away."

Percy Bysshe Shelley

THINKING IT OVER

(1) Who was Ozymandias? _____

_____

· (2) Explain what line 6 means, "Tell that its sculptor well those passions read." _____

_____

STUDYING THE PASSAGE

(1) Find the Main Idea: Choose one answer.
   (a) One can learn about life by traveling.
   (b) We have learned from experience that people should not strive for material greatness because it always involves the adoption of greed, hate, and lust for power.
   (c) Time and nature eventually destroy or reduce to insignificance all that is materially great to human beings.
   (d) Ozymandias got what he deserved. _____

*Shelley lived from 1792–1822.

(2) Find the Facts: Mark each one *true* or *false*.
  (a) Ozymandias was apparently a powerful king.   (a) _____
  (b) The "I" in line one refers to the poet.   (b) _____
  (c) "The hand" in line eight refers to the hand of the sculptor.   (c) _____
  (d) The "heart" in line eight refers to the heart of Ozymandias.   (d) _____
  (e) Shelley never saw the statue of Ozymandias.   (e) _____
  (f) The sculptor hated Ozymandias.   (f) _____
  (g) The statue remains in good condition.   (g) _____
  (h) The poem indicates that the people around Ozymandias rose up against the
      injustices of the king and put in a more just and humane ruler.   (h) _____

(3) Find the Order: Number the following in the order in which they appear in the passage.
  (a) The lone and level sands stretch far away.   (a) _____
  (b) I met a traveler from an antique land.   (b) _____
  (c) On the pedestal these words appear.   (c) _____
  (d) Two vast and trunkless legs of stone stand in the desert.   (d) _____
  (e) Nothing beside remains.   (e) _____
  (f) The statue had a frown and a wrinkled lip.   (f) _____
  (g) "Look on my works, ye Mighty, and despair."   (g) _____

(4) Go beyond the Facts: As it relates to the rest of the poem, what does line eight mean?
  (a) Ozymandias had to be fed by a slave.
  (b) The sculptor made his living by working for the king.
  (c) The king fed on mockery.
  (d) The sculptor's work showed his disapproval of the evil passions of Ozymandias.   _____

(5) Which *one* of the following is *not* an image of decay in the poem?
  (a) Antique land.
  (b) Trunkless legs.
  (c) Shattered visage.
  (d) Wrinkled lip.   _____

USING THE WORDS

(1) Words and Their Meanings: Find the boldfaced word for these definitions. One word has *two* meanings.

  _____   (a) a work of art from an earlier period

  _____   (b) face (of a person or animal)

  _____   (c) base or foundation

  _____   (d) ancient

  _____   (e) to remain alive, to endure

  _____   (f) a facial expression of contempt

  _____   (g) an artist who carves (usually in wood or stone)

  _____   (h) broken into pieces

  _____   (i) treated with contempt or ridicule

(2) Write a paragraph using three of the words from the list above. Use a separate piece of paper.

WRITING ABOUT IT

Use a separate piece of paper.

(1) Analyze what the poet is saying in "Ozymandias" and then put the poem into your own words. Be sure to include: a description of what the statue looks like now, the character of the person revealed in the face of the statue, and the message of the poem.

(2) This poem may be as appropriate today as it was over a hundred years ago. Why?

KOKO'S HOME*

ABOUT THE PASSAGE   This passage describes the home of Koko—the gorilla you read about in Selection 2. Here, Francine Patterson, Koko's teacher and the author of this selection, describes Koko's routine to give you a clearer picture of the kind of life the gorilla lives.

REASON FOR READING   Read this passage quickly to improve your speed. Concentrate on the specific facts and details as well as general ideas, so your comprehension is not lost as you speed up your reading.

READ THE PASSAGE

Koko's mobile home, situated on the Stanford University campus, came to us with normal accommodations—a kitchen, a living room, and a hallway leading to a small bedroom, bathroom, and master bedroom. Chain-link panels now protect the living room windows and large sliding glass doors from Koko's enthusiastic pounding. The living room became Koko's nursery with the **installation** of her metal sleeping box, an exercise bar, and a trapeze. Familiar household items stock the trailer: toys, books, pots and pans, chairs, mirrors, a refrigerator, stove, sink, and bed.

After our second gorilla, the young, male Michael arrived, we transformed the master bedroom into a second training playroom with a dangling chain, a swing, and a bench. The bathroom became a separate kitchen for Michael.

Two solid-wood doors separate Michael's **domain** from Koko's. With these doors open, one large common play area is formed for daily exercise sessions and visits.

Because of her sharp teeth and endless curiosity about how things are constructed, Koko has never had a bed with a mattress. Instead, she makes a nest using towels with a variety of underpinnings. Currently she has settled on a comfortable (I've tried it!) nest of two **plush** rugs draped over a motorcycle tire.

Koko rises at 8 or 8:30 in the morning, when my assistant Ann Southcombe and I arrive—that is, if she hasn't been **roused** earlier by Michael's morning antics. Following a breakfast of cereal or raisin-thick rice bread with milk and fruit, Koko helps with the daily cleaning of her room. She also thoroughly enjoys going over Michael's room with a sponge. Unfortunately, Koko usually rips the sponge to shreds when supervision slackens.

Then, most mornings, Koko sits before the electric typewriter keyboard in the kitchen for a thirty-minute lesson in **auditory** English. Wearying of this, Koko asks me, "Have Mike in?"

About an hour is taken up with Koko and Michael's tickling, tumbling, wrestling, chasing, and playing games or hide-and-seek. I usually leave during their banana and milk snack. Then my assistant gives Koko her regular sign language instruction.

Koko has a light meal—an egg or meat, juice, and a vitamin tablet—at 1 p.m. and a sandwich (usually peanut butter and jam) at 2 p.m. or 2:30. Most days I return at 3 p.m. and either sample Koko's signing on videotape, invite Mike in for another play session, or take them out for a walk or a drive.

Dinner at 5 p.m. consists almost **exclusively** of fresh vegetables. Koko's top preferences are corn on the cob and tomatoes; her lowest, spinach and

*From "Conversations with a Gorilla" by Francine Patterson in *National Geographic,* vol. 154, no. 4, October 1978. Reprinted by permission of the National Geographic Society.

carrots. She also dabbles in **gourmet** vegetables such as artichokes, asparagus, and eggplant. She absolutely **abhors** olives, mushrooms, and radishes. If Koko cleans her plate, she gets dessert—usually Jell-O, dried fruits, a cookie, or cheese and a cracker.

After dinner Koko may engage in a private **monologue** as she relaxes with a book or magazine, and while fingering a picture, she signs, "There flower"; or as she nests with her blankets, "That soft"; or as she plays with her dolls, "That ear," placing the doll's ear against her own. Some evenings she asks if she may visit Michael's quarters.

Following toothbrushing and application of baby oil, both gorillas settle down about 7 or 7:30 p.m. with a "night dish." This is a small fruit treat designed to make bedtime a more pleasant experience; for most nights, Koko cries when I leave her.

THINKING IT OVER

(1) What is Koko's home? _____

(2) Why does Koko live this kind of life? _____

_____

_____

STUDYING THE PASSAGE

(1) Find the Main Idea: Choose one answer.
  (a) How Koko was trained to live in a home.
  (b) How Koko came to share her home.
  (c) Koko's home and lifestyle.
  (d) The antics of Koko.   _____

(2) Find the Facts: Mark each one *true* or *false*.
  (a) The livingroom became Koko's nursery.   (a) _____
  (b) Koko lives in a mobile home originally designed for human beings.   (b) _____
  (c) Chain-link panels separate Koko's and Michael's living quarters.   (c) _____
  (d) Koko helps with the daily cleaning.   (d) _____
  (e) Koko has a banana and milk at 1:00 p.m.   (e) _____
  (f) Koko's favorite vegetables are corn on the cob and tomatoes.   (f) _____
  (g) Koko has her dinner at 5:00 p.m.   (g) _____
  (h) Koko gets dessert only if she cleans her plate.   (h) _____

(3) Find the Order: Number the following in the order in which they appear in the passage.
  (a) Most days I return at 3 p.m.   (a) _____
  (b) Familiar household items stock the trailer.   (b) _____
  (c) Most mornings Koko sits before the electric typewriter.   (c) _____
  (d) We transformed the master bedroom into a second training playroom. (d) _____
  (e) Most nights Koko cries when I leave her.   (e) _____
  (f) Koko enjoys going over Michael's room with a sponge.   (f) _____
  (g) After dinner Koko may engage in a private monologue as she relaxes with a book. (g) _____
  (h) Because of her sharp teeth and endless curiosity about how things are constructed, Koko has never had a bed with a mattress.   (h) _____

(4) Go beyond the Facts: Which *two* of the following can you conclude from the passage?
   (a) Koko has a great deal of freedom.
   (b) Koko's life is structured and regulated.
   (c) Koko's day is not all that different from a child's.
   (d) Koko's home is not at all like that of a human. ____ ____

(5) Determine the Writer's Style and Technique: From which of the following is this passage taken?
   (a) A novel.
   (b) A short story.
   (c) An article.
   (d) A scientific report. ____

USING THE WORDS

(1) Words and Their Meanings: Find the boldfaced word for these definitions.

   _____ (a) hates

   _____ (b) a long speech or talk made by one person

   _____ (c) having a thick, deep pile

   _____ (d) a setting up; putting in place

   _____ (e) experienced through hearing

   _____ (f) living quarters; territory

   _____ (g) solely, excluding everything else

   _____ (h) prized by those with especially fine taste in food

   _____ (i) awakened; moved to activity

(2) Write a paragraph using three of the words from the list above. Use a separate piece of paper.

WRITING ABOUT IT

Use a separate piece of paper.

(1) Koko is obviously a smart gorilla who has been taught to communicate with humans. Take Koko's development a little further, and have her write an entry in her diary describing her day from *her* point of view.

(2) Describe an unusual house. It can be one you are acquainted with or one you make up. Be sure to be very specific. Include concrete examples and details as the writer does in the passage about Koko's home.

70

LOUISA MAY ALCOTT*

ABOUT THE PASSAGE   This selection is taken from the award-winning biography, *Invincible Louisa* by Cornelia Meigs. The author describes how Louisa Alcott used people and places from her personal experiences in her novels, especially *Little Women*, the story of the March family and its girls, Meg, Jo, Beth, and Amy.

You will better understand the excerpt if you know that Abba May was Louisa's mother; Anna, Elizabeth, and May were Louisa's sisters.

REASON FOR READING   To learn about Louisa's life and work.

READ THE PASSAGE

In the rather shadowy figure of the March girls' father, it is hard to recognize Bronson Alcott. Louisa always meant to write a book that should have her father as the central character; she spoke of it by various names, "The Cost of An Idea" or "An Old-Fashioned Boy." She had thought of it and spoken of it long before she **undertook** "Little Women." She was so unlike Bronson, that, although she was devoted to him, there were certain of his ideas that she did not quite **fathom** the motives that lay behind them. She waited all of her life for the moment when she really would understand him fully; and she waited too long, for the book was never written. Perhaps it was because she had this plan still in view that she did not make a more **striking** figure out of the father of Meg, Jo, Beth, and Amy. But in one matter, we see her true affection for him coming into the very center of the stage.

The real power of the book, however, centers upon Jo. She was Louisa to the life, more so, perhaps, than the author ever dreamed of making her. Louisa's honest opinion of herself was so very humble that she made not the slightest effort to dress up her **counterpart** in the **semblance** of a **conventional** heroine. Her picture of Jo is the farthest thing removed from **flattery**. She has told frankly of every drawback in her appearance and her nature, her round shoulders, her long-limbed awkwardness, her thorny moods, her headlong mistakes, her quick flashes of temper. Yet Jo is lovable beyond words and more real than any of the others. She is real because Louisa understood her even better than the rest; she stands out from the background because Louisa herself was such a magnificent character that a truthful study of her becomes, without any intention, a splendid figure also.

Louisa's kind but outwardly severe grandfather, known only during the Temple School period of their life in Boston, was put into the book as Mr. Lawrence, the grandfather of Laurie. She has declared that "Aunt March is no one," but her family say otherwise. They all see in that **autocratically** generous lady the reflection of no other than the great Aunt Hancock, with her connections in high places, her family tyranny and her good heart. Louisa could not remember her, but the family legend was enough, and Aunt Hancock lives on in thoroughly Aunt Hancockish fashion. In some of the kind relatives who were so kind to Jo and Amy we surely see good Cousin

*From *Invincible Louisa*, by Cornelia Meigs. Copyright © 1933, 1961, 1968 by Cornelia Meigs. Reprinted with permission of Little, Brown and Company.

Lizzie Wells. Not all of the minor figures can be traced to their originals, but it is safe to say that they all lived and that Louisa knew them.

With *Little Women*, Louisa achieved what she really wanted, a piece of work that she actually knew to be her best. With it she achieved also the appreciation of the world and such prosperity as gave her full power, at last, to do just what she wished. It is delightful to read of how her name came to be on every tongue; how she grew to be not merely famous, which mattered much. After all the years of doubting her own powers, of looking for her true field, of thinking of herself as a struggling failure, she was obliged at last to admit, even in the depths of her own soul, that she was a success.

THINKING IT OVER

(1) Where did Louisa Alcott get the material to write *Little Women*? _____

_____

(2) Who is Jo? _____

_____

(3) What was unusual about the way Louisa Alcott depicted her heroine? _____

_____

_____

STUDYING THE PASSAGE

(1) Find the Main Idea: Choose one answer.
   (a) Louisa Alcott's life as a child.
   (b) Where Louisa Alcott lived during her childhood.
   (c) All about Louisa Alcott's famly.
   (d) All about the book Louisa Alcott wrote.   _____

(2) Find the Facts: Mark each of these *true* or *false*.
   (a) The "Cost of an Idea" was published before "Little Women."   (a) _____
   (b) Louisa was unlike her father.   (b) _____
   (c) Louisa fully understood her father's ideas.   (c) _____
   (d) Jo was the heroine in the book.   (d) _____
   (e) Louisa put her grandfather into the book.   (e) _____
   (f) There is no indication in this selection whether Louisa put her father
       in the book.   (f) _____
   (g) Louisa was dissatisfied with her book.   (g) _____
   (h) The book made her famous.   (h) _____

(3) Find the Order: Number the following in the order in which they appear in the passage.
   (a) She was a success.   (a) _____
   (b) Louisa meant to write a book in which her father is the central character. (b) _____
   (c) Not all the minor figures can be traced to their originals.   (c) _____
   (d) There were certain of his ideas that she did not quite fathom. (d) _____
   (e) Yet Jo is lovable beyond words.   (e) _____
   (f) She has declared that "Aunt March is no one."   (f) _____

(g) The real power of the book, however, centers upon Jo. (g) _____

(h) In the shadowy figure of the March girls' father, it's hard to recognize Bronson Alcott. (h) _____

(4) Go beyond the Facts: Choose one answer.
    (a) The four Alcott sisters were the models for the four March sisters.
    (b) Louisa Alcott was conceited.
    (c) The four Alcott sisters were not very close.
    (d) Louisa was probably an insensitive person. _____

(5) Determine the Writer's Style and Technique: What *one* method does Ms. Meigs use in the excerpt?
    (a) Comparison.
    (b) Examples.
    (c) A series of events.
    (d) One particular incident in Louisa Alcott's life. _____

USING THE WORDS

(1) Words and Their Meaning: Find the boldfaced word for these definitions. One word has two meanings.

_____ (a) one who closely or exactly resembles another

_____ (b) the act of portraying favorably

_____ (c) to understand completely

_____ (d) possessing an unusual or remarkable quality

_____ (e) entered into or upon a task

_____ (f) with unlimited authority or power

_____ (g) likeness

_____ (h) conforming to accepted standards

_____ (i) the act of complimenting excessively

(2) Write a paragraph using three of the vocabulary words. Use a separate piece of paper.

WRITING ABOUT IT

Use a separate piece of paper.

(1) Find out about an author you enjoy. Then write a short biography of him or her.

(2) Write about an incident that has happened to you as though it had happened to someone else. Have your character react as you would and express your thoughts and feelings.

Selection 23—Subject: Literature and Language
Theme: Different Literary Forms and Styles

THE WALTZ

ABOUT THE PASSAGE   If portions of this story were used in isolation, you would probably have a very different impression of the character and situation that Dorothy Parker, the author, has described.

REASON FOR READING   To read a longer literary passage. Note the author's clever use of words.

READ THE PASSAGE

Why, thank you so much, I'd adore to. I don't want to dance with him. I don't want to dance with anybody. And even if I did, it wouldn't be him. He'd be well down among the last ten. I've seen the way he dances; it looks like something you do on St. Walpurgis Night.[1] Just think, not a quarter of an hour ago, here I was sitting, feeling so sorry for the poor girl he was dancing with. And now *I'm* going to be the poor girl. Well, well. Isn't it a small world?

And a peach of a world, too. A true little corker. Its events are so fascinating unpredictable, are they not? Here I was, minding my own business, not doing a stitch of harm to any living soul. And then he comes into my life, all smiles and city manners, to sue me for the favor of one memorable mazurka.[2] Why, he scarcely knows my name, let alone what it stands for. It stands for Despair, Bewilderment. Futility, Degradation, and **Premeditated** Murder, but little does he wot.[3] I don't wot his name either; I haven't any idea what it is. Jukes, would be my guess from the look in his eyes. How do you do, Mr. Jukes? And how is that dear little brother of yours, with the two heads?

Ah, now why does he have to come around me, with his low requests? Why can't he let me lead my own life? I ask so little—just to be left alone in my quiet corner of the table, to do my evening brooding over all my sorrows. And he

must come, with his bows and his scrapes and his may-I-have-this-ones. And I had to go and tell him that I'd adore to dance with him. I cannot understand why I wasn't struck right down dead. Yes, and being struck dead would look like a day in the country, compared to struggling out a dance with this boy. But what could I do? Everyone else at the table had got up to dance, except him and me. There I was, trapped. Trapped like a trap in a trap.

What can you say, when a man asks you to dance with him? I most certainly will *not* dance with you, I'll see you in hell first. Oh, yes, *do* let's dance together—it's so nice to meet a man who isn't a scaredy-cat about catching my beri-beri.[4] No. There was nothing for me to do, but say I'd adore to. Well, we might as well get it over with. All right, Cannonball, let's run out on the field. You won the toss; you can lead.

Why, I think it's more of a waltz, really. Isn't it? We might just listen to the music a second. Shall we? Oh, yes, it's a waltz. Mind? Why, I'm simply thrilled. I'd love to waltz with you.

I'd love to waltz with you. I'd love to waltz with you. I'd love to have my tonsils out, I'd love to be in a midnight fire at sea. Well, it's too late now. We're getting under way. *Oh.* Oh, dear. Oh, dear, dear, dear. Oh, this is even worse than you thought it was going to be. Oh, if I had had any real grasp of what this dance would be like, I'd have held out for sitting it out. Well, it will proba-

[1] When witches meet to celebrate their Sabbath on the highest peak of the Harz Mountains—from a German legend.

[2] A polish fold dance.

[3] Know

[4] A disease caused by a vitamin deficiency; common in the late 1800's.

bly amount to the same thing in the end. We'll be sitting it out on the floor in a minute, if he keeps this up.

I'm so glad I brought it to his attention that this is a waltz they're playing. Heaven knows what might have happened, if he had thought it was something fast; we'd have blown the sides right out of the building. Why does he always want to be somewhere that he isn't? Why can't we stay in one place just long enough to get **acclimated**? It's this constant rush, rush, rush, that's the curse of American life. That's the reason that we're all of us so —*Ow!* Don't *kick*, you idiot; this is only second down. Oh, my shin. My poor, poor shin, that I've had ever since I was a little girl!

Oh, no, no, no. Goodness, no. It didn't hurt the least little bit. And anyway it was my fault. Really it was. Truly. Well, you're just being sweet, to say that. It really was all my fault.

I wonder what I'd better do—kill him this instant, with my naked hands, or wait and let him drop in his traces.[5] May be it's best not to make a scene. I guess I'll just lie low, and watch the pace get him. He can't keep this up indefinitely—he's only flesh and blood. Die he must, and die he shall, for what he did to me. I don't want to be of the oversensitive type, but you can't tell me that kick was unpremeditated. Freud says there are no accidents. I've led no cloistered life, I've known dancing partners who have spoiled my slippers and torn my dress; but when it comes to kicking, I am Outraged Womanhood. When you kick me in the shin, *smile*.

Maybe he didn't do it **maliciously**. Maybe it's just his way of showing his high spirits. I suppose I ought to be glad that one of us is having such a good time. I suppose I ought to think myself lucky if he brings me back alive. Maybe it's **captious** to demand of a practically strange man that he leave your shins as he found them. After all, the poor boy's doing the best he can. Probably he grew up in the hill country, and never had no larnin'. I bet they had to throw him on his back to get shoes on him.

Yes, it's lovely isn't it? It's simply lovely. It's the loveliest waltz. Isn't it? Oh, I think it's lovely, too.

Why, I'm getting positively drawn to the Triple Threat here. He's my hero. He has the heart of a lion, and the sinews of a buffalo. Look at him—never a thought of the consequences, never afraid of his face, hurling himself into every scrimmage, eyes shining, cheeks ablaze. And shall it be said that I hung back? No, a thousand times no. What's it to me if I have to spend the next couple of years in a plaster cast? Come on, Butch, right through them! Who wants to live forever?

Oh. Oh, dear. Oh, he's all right, thank goodness. For a while I thought they'd have to carry him off the field. Ah, I couldn't bear to have anything happen to him. I love him. I love him better than anybody in the world. Look at the spirit he gets into a dreary, commonplace waltz; how **effete** the other dancers seem, beside him. He is youth and vigor and courage, he is strength and gayety and—*Ow!* Get off my instep, you hulking peasant! What do you think I am, anyway—a gangplank? *Ow!*

No, of course it didn't hurt. Why, it didn't a bit. Honestly. And it was all my fault. You see, that little step of yours—well, it's perfectly lovely, but it's just a tiny bit tricky to follow at first. Oh, did you work it up yourself? You really did? Well, aren't you amazing! Oh, now I think I've got it. Oh, I think it's lovely. I was watching you do it when you were dancing before. It's awfully effective when you look at it.

It's awfully effective when you look at it. I bet I'm awfully effective when you look at me. My hair is hanging along my cheeks, my shirt is swaddles about me, I can feel the cold damp of my brow. I must look like something out of the Fall of the House of Usher. This sort of thing takes a fearful toll of a woman my age. And he worked up his little step himself, he with his **degenerate** cunning. And it was just a tiny bit tricky at first, but now I think I've got it. Two stumbles, slip, and a twenty-yard dash; yes, I've

[5]Part of a harness that attaches a horse to something to be drawn.

75

got it. I've got several other things, too, including a split shin and a bitter heart. I hate this creature I'm chained to. I hated him the moment I saw his leering, **bestial** face. And here I've been locked in his **noxious** embrace for the thirty-five years this waltz has lasted. Is that orchestra never going to stop playing? Or must his obscene travesty of a dance go on until hell burns out?

Oh, they're going to play another encore. Oh, goody. Oh, that's lovely. Tired? I should say I'm not tired. I'd like to go on like this forever.

I should say I'm not tired. I'm dead, that's all I am. Dead, and in what a cause! And the music is never going to stop playing, and we're going on like this, Double-Time Charlie and I, throughout eternity. I suppose I won't care any more, after this first hundred thousand years. I suppose nothing will matter then, not heat nor pain nor broken heart nor cruel, aching weariness. Well. It can't come too soon for me.

I wonder why I didn't tell him I was tired. I wonder why I didn't suggest going back to the table. I could have said let's just listen to the music. Yes, and if he would, that would be the first bit of attention he has given it all evening. George Jean Nathan said that the lovely rhythms of the waltz should be listened to in stillness and not be accompanied by strange **gyrations** of the human body. I think that's what he said. I think it was George Jean Nathan. Anyhow, whatever he said and whoever he was and whatever he's doing now, he's better off than I am. That's safe. Any-body who isn't waltzing with this Mrs. O'Leary's cow I've got here is having a good time.

Still, if we were back at the table, I'd probably have to talk to him. Look at him—what could you say to a thing like that! Did you go to the circus this year, what's your favorite kind of ice cream, how do you spell cat? I guess I'm as well off here. As well off as if I were in a cement mixer in full action.

I'm past all feeling now. The only way I can tell when he steps on me is that I can hear the splintering of bones. And all the events of my life are passing before my eyes. There was the time I was in a hurricane in the West Indies, there was the day I got my head cut open in the taxi smash, there was the night the drunken lady threw a bronze ash-tray at her own true love and got me instead, there was that summer that the sailboat kept capsizing.[7] Ah, what an easy, peaceful time was mine, until I fell in with Swifty, here, I didn't know what trouble was, before I got drawn into this *danse macabre.*[8] I think my mind is beginning to wander. It almost seems to me as if the orchestra were stopping. It couldn't be, of course; it could never, never be. And yet in my ears there is a silence like the sound of angel voices. . . .

Oh, they've stopped, the mean things. They're not going to play anymore. Oh, darn. Oh, do you think they would? Do you really think so, if you gave them fifty dollars? Oh, that would be lovely. And look, do tell them to play this same thing. I'd simply adore to go on waltzing.[9]

THINKING IT OVER

(1) What is Dorothy Parker's purpose?
    (a) To shock the reader.
    (b) To amuse the reader.
    (c) To persuade the reader.
    (d) To deceive the reader.

_____

[7]Overturning.

[8]Dance of death, a symbolic dance in which Death leads people to their grave.

[9]"The Waltz" from *The Portable Dorothy Parker*. © 1933, 1961 by Dorothy Parker. Reprinted by permission of Viking Penguin Inc.

(2) What kind of person does the writer say her partner is? Give three traits the writer implies.

    (a) _____

    (b) _____

    (c) _____

(3) What name does she give him? _____

    Why is this name appropriate? _____

(4) Throughout the account Dorothy Parker compares her situation to something. What is this?

_____

STUDYING THE PASSAGE

(1) Find the Main Idea: Choose one.
    (a) The pitfalls of dancing with a poor partner.
    (b) What to do when dancing with a poor partner.
    (c) Reactions to dancing with a poor partner.
    (d) How to avoid dancing with a poor partner.   _____

(2) Find the Facts: Mark each one of these *true* or *false*.
    (a) The writer agrees to dance since she does not want to hurt the man's feelings.   (a) _____
    (b) She describes him as having two heads.   (b) _____
    (c) Parker says the dancing is worse than she thought it would be.   (c) _____
    (d) She had known her partner for some time.   (d) _____
    (e) She refers to her partner as being a country person.   (e) _____
    (f) Her partner bruised her arm badly.   (f) _____
    (g) They are learning to dance a new step.   (g) _____
    (h) She prolongs her agony through her own free will.   (h) _____

(3) Find the Order: Number the following in the order in which they appear in the passage.
    (a) I wonder what I'd better do—kill him this instant . . .   (a) _____
    (b) And now *I'm* going to be the poor girl.   (b) _____
    (c) He's my hero.   (c) _____
    (d) Why can't he let me lead my own life?   (d) _____
    (e) . . . well it's perfectly lovely, but it's just a tiny bit tricky to follow at first.   (e) _____
    (f) And all the events of my life are passing before my eyes.   (f) _____
    (g) I suppose I won't care anymore, after the first hundred thousand years.   (g) _____
    (h) We'll be sitting it out on the floor in a minute, if he keeps this up.   (h) _____

(4) Go beyond the Facts: Which *one* of the following is Dorothy Parker implying that people are?
    (a) frank
    (b) hypocritical
    (c) poor dancers
    (d) too sensitive   _____

(5) Determine the Writer's Style and Technique: Which *one* of the following does Dorothy Parker *not* do to tell her story?
    (a) Reveals the character by showing negative aspects.

(b) Uses exaggeration to make her point.

(c) Gives the facts succinctly in a forthright manner.

(d) Uses words with the opposite meaning to what she is actually saying. _____

USING THE WORDS

(1) Words and Their Meanings: Find the boldfaced word for these definitions.

_____ (a) adapted to a new environment or condition

_____ (b) considered or planned beforehand

_____ (c) having sunk into a lower or worse condition.

_____ (d) spiraling, revolving, curving movements

_____ (e) fault finding; hypercritical; carping

_____ (f) hurtful; unwholesome

_____ (g) beast-like

_____ (h) wornout from use

_____ (i) with evil intent

(2) Write a paragraph using three of the words from the list above. Use a separate piece of paper.

WRITING ABOUT IT

Use a separate piece of paper.

(1) Write a story about a memorable experience you had dancing with someone you did not know. Use a literary style similar to the author's to express both your feelings and those of your partner.

(2) Create a conversation in which one person says the opposite of what they mean. Choose a partner to have this conversation with, and discuss what it felt like.

THE MYSTERY OF MANDALAS

ABOUT THE PASSAGE   Did you know that there is a pattern or picture that you and other people in the world have made? What do you think it is?

REASON FOR READING   To follow an explanation of an unusual, but often drawn, art design.

READ THE PASSAGE

Art expresses a person's feelings or ideas. One form of art has appeared for thousands of years in hundreds of different cultures. In fact, it appears that people naturally, even unconsciously, are moved to draw it. This is the mandala (MAN da la), drawn by people of all ages—even today.

Children love to draw pictures. Whether they live in the United States, China, Africa, or Australia, the first drawings children make are scribbles. After they have drawn scribbles for a while, putting the scribbles in different places and in different patterns on the page, they invariably draw a circle with an X or cross in it. This is the basic form of the mandala. Why do children cross-culturally draw this particular image at this developmental stage of drawing? The answer is unknown.

The word *mandala* comes from a word used in India to mean "circle," which is what a mandala is—a circle. It is really much more than that. An examination of art from various countries and time periods reveals that the circle (egg or sphere) is often elaborated on in order to make a flower or a wheel, sometimes even a wheel in rotation. The circle may have a castle, city, or courtyard **motif** divided into four parts, or the mandala may look like an eye, complete with pupil and iris. The cen-  ter of a mandala is often a star, sun, or cross, generally with four, eight, or twelve rays. Sometimes the circle is represented by a snake or fish coiled in the center to make a spiral shape. Mandalas often have a circle and a square together. These are usually **symmetrical**, with either the circle or the square inside one another, and often relate the number four.

There are a surprising number of things in our culture that have the basic mandala design. Picture the sign for a railroad crossing, or the design on the face of a clock. It is divided into twelve parts, just as many mandalas are. Picture the grid of a radar screen, or the design of a compass with its four major directions. Different cultures throughout history have identified these four directions in relation to a circle. Why four divisions of a circle? The answer is unknown.

Why do we have names for only four specific times in a day (which is often thought of as a circle): sunrise, noon, sunset, and midnight? Why are there four seasons in the circle of the year—spring, summer, fall, and winter? The earth makes a circle around the sun, and there are special names for four points in this circle: the summer and winter solstices, and the spring and fall **equinoxes.** Maybe all of these things are merely **coincidences**; but there is something rather mysterious about it, something almost magical.

Mandalas are often found in religious art. The stained-glass rose windows in gothic cathedrals, like Notre Dame in Paris, are mandalas. Crucifixes are often placed in circles. There are Navajo sand-painting mandalas and ancient Egyptian and Roman mandalas.

Throughout history mandalas have been drawn depicting religious experiences. **Mystics** have often drawn mandalas to express the relationship between God and human beings. Buddhists and Hindus use mandalas in **meditation.** Their pictures, drawn on temple walls or on cloth, are meant to represent the nature of the universe in relation to a person's soul. Colorful and elaborate deities or divine symbols are designed to represent the various forces of the universe.

The psychologist Carl Jung studied mandalas and was responsible for making the modern western world aware of their existence and meaning.

Jung believed that drawing mandalas was a means of expressing what was deepest in a person's mind. Jung studied mandalas drawn by others. He observed that people who casually, **spontaneously** drew mandalas could learn a great deal about themselves. But people who consciously planned their designs learned nothing.

Mandalas are often beautiful, and their meanings are fascinating. If you would like to find out more about them, or if you would like to look at a series of mandalas drawn by one person, read the last two essays in Jung's *Archetypes and the Collective Unconscious.**

From *Man, Myth, and Magic, an Encyclopedia of the Supernatural* by Mildred Byrd. New York: Criterion Books, 1969.

THINKING IT OVER

(1) Give three reasons that people make mandalas.

(a) _____

(b) _____

(c) _____

(2) Name three things that have the mandala shape.

(a) _____

(b) _____

(c) _____

STUDYING THE PASSAGE

(1) Find the Main Idea: Choose one answer.
    (a) Children in Australia draw mandalas.
    (b) What mandalas are and why people make them.
    (c) The origin of our clock face.
    (d) Mandalas: a study of their history. _____

*Carl G. Jung, *Archetypes and the Collective Unconscious*. Collected Words vol. 9, pt. 1, 2nd ed. Princeton University Press, 1969.

(2) Find the Facts: Mark each one *true* or *false*.
    (a) Mandalas are musical instruments used in India.   (a) _____

    (b) All children draw mandalas while they are learning to draw.   (b) _____

    (c) Mandalas often bring together the circle and the square.   (c) _____

    (d) Sometimes mandalas look as if they are turning.   (d) _____

    (e) Mandalas are attempts to draw pictures of what a day looks like. (e) _____

    (f) Mandalas are drawn only by people who have unusual experiences. (f) _____

    (g) Mandalas usually relate the numbers two and three to each other. (g) _____

    (h) Jung observed that people who draw mandalas spontaneously could learn a lot
        from them.   (h) _____

(3) Find the Order: Number the following in the order in which they appear in the passage.
    (a) We don't know why humans tend to make four divisions in a circle. (a) _____

    (b) They are often beautiful, and their meanings can be fascinating. (b) _____

    (c) The pictures represent the nature of the whole universe and its relation to a
        person's soul.   (c) _____

    (d) Mystics have often drawn mandalas.   (d) _____

    (e) The center of a mandala is often a star, sun, or cross.   (e) _____

    (f) Why are there four seasons in the circle of the year?   (f) _____

    (g) All children draw mandalas.   (g) _____

    (h) Think of the sign for a railroad crossing.   (h) _____

(4) Go beyond the Facts: Which *one* of the following is the basic mandala shape?
    (a) The top of a Phillips-head screw seen from above.

    (b) The eye of a needle.

    (c) A picture window.

    (d) A demon's foot.   _____

(5) Determine the Writer's Style and Technique: Choose one answer.
    (a) Appeals to your emotions.

    (b) Gives scientific evidence in a logical argument.

    (c) Gives many examples to show what something is.

    (d) Criticizes or judges a work of art.   _____

USING THE WORDS

(1) Words and Their Meanings: Find the boldfaced word for these definitions.

_____ (a) central theme or idea, repeated design

_____ (b) the two days in each year when the day and night are exactly the same length

_____ (c) a group of events or circumstances linked together for no apparent reason; remarkable correspondences or similarities

_____ (d) people who believe that they communicate directly with God or ultimate reality

_____ (e) a private spiritual exercise consisting of steady concentration on a single point, process, idea, or paradox

_____ (f) balanced, even; the same on both sides of the center, as in a design

_____ (g) freely, naturally; on impulse

(2) Write a paragraph using three of the words from the list above. Use a separate piece of paper.

WRITING ABOUT IT

Use a separate piece of paper.

(1) Reread the passage and underline the topic sentences in one color and the details in another color. Then make an outline of the passage.

(2) Choose any topic you wish to write about. Make notes and organize them into main ideas or categories. Next, write a topic sentence for each main idea or category. Then develop each topic sentence into a paragraph by including the necessary facts, details, and examples. Finally, write up each paragraph, edit, and write your final copy.

A MYSTERIOUS POET: EMILY DICKINSON

ABOUT THE PASSAGE   Emily Dickinson was a mysterious woman. In her early thirties she permanently secluded herself from the world. After her death, the discovery of over one thousand poems, which she had written, revealed two important things—she was a deep and intense person, and one of America's greatest **lyric** poets.

REASON FOR READING   To learn about a major figure in American literature.

READ THE PASSAGE

Emily Dickinson was born on December 10, 1830 in Amherst, then a picturesque country town in western Massachusetts. She spent most of her life there, living with her strong-willed father; her quiet mother; her brother, Austin; and her sister, Lavinia.

Emily had a happy, carefree childhood. Her family lived in a large, comfortable house with a pleasant garden, which was one of Emily's lifetime joys. She grew up to be bright, personable, and lively, conversing effortlessly and wittily with many household visitors, including a number of important writers of the period.

She was very close to Austin and Lavinia, and spent happy hours sharing confidences with them. She was particularly attached to her stern father, even though she was also afraid of him. Once she told a friend, "I never knew how to tell time by the clock till I was fifteen. My father thought he had taught me, but I did not understand, and I was afraid to say I did not, and afraid to ask anyone else, lest he should know."

Emily's education began in the local public school where all the children, whatever their ages, learned together. When she was eleven, she went to Amherst Academy. She has said that the years she spent there were the happiest of her childhood. Emily proved to be an **apt**, hardworking, and enthusiastic student, although poor health prevented her from attending class regularly.

In September 1847, Emily's father sent her to Mount Holyoke Seminary, a well-known college some miles from home. At college, however, she was homesick; she missed her family and home surroundings. Because of the strong religious influence of the school's head, Mary Lyon, she experienced many **anguished**, soul-searching sessions about her feelings toward God and life. Emily maintained her independence, rejecting much of the rigid religion of her generation.

In her teens, Emily was a young woman with glorious auburn hair parted in the middle and pulled straight back in a net behind her head. Its color was, to quote Emily, "like the sherry in the glass that the guest leaves." She had many friends and enjoyed life, once even daring to have a dance in the living room when her strict, religious parents were not at home.

Emily loved nature and long walks with her dog, especially in the fall when the hills, she said, "put on their **paisley** shawls." Her happiness is captured in quotes such as, "I find **ecstasy** in living; the mere sense of living is joy enough."

Emily certainly loved books. She read widely; Emerson, Shakespeare, the Bible, the Brontes, the liberal books of Lydia Maria Child, and Harriet Beecher Stowe's *Uncle Tom's Cabin*. Most of all she loved poetry. She began to write poems—many of them on odd scraps of paper or whatever was handy. She usually wrote at night, after the family had gone to bed and it was quiet.

She was fascinated with words and was always consulting the dictionary. She wrote and rewrote phrases and lines until they expressed the **precise** thought or feeling she had in mind. When she was happy with them, she put them into hand-sewn booklets, which she kept in a bureau drawer. She wrote them purely for her own satisfaction, and apart from the ones she included in letters to her family and friends, she had no intention of them being read. It was only after her death in 1886, that the world discovered that she had written over 1200 poems.

In her early thirties, Emily's behavior changed dramatically. From that period, until her death in 1886, she withdrew from the world. She **shunned** all but her closest family, and confined herself to her house and garden. She would disappear upstairs when company arrived. In addition, she began to wear only white dresses. Some explain her strange behavior by insisting that Emily was twice disappointed in love, and that her pain was so intense, that she died to the world, and expressed her passion only in poetry. They see her poems on love and separation, and her eternal-bride image as support for this explanation. Others reject this idea as a romantic legend, contending that not enough of her poetry and biographical data uphold such an explanation.

Emily developed a style of writing unique for her time, and today her poems are praised for their original metaphors, brilliant imagery, and effective use of **paradox.** In her **succinct** poems, Emily spoke of ordinary occurrences in a fresh and striking way. Her main themes were of nature, human experience, eternity, and death. Like the poet herself, they were sometimes filled with anger, anguish, and rebellion, and at other times with warmth, wonder, and wit.

THINKING IT OVER

(1) What facts present the greatest contrast in the story of Emily's life? _____

_____

(2) Name three common themes in Emily Dickinson's poems.

    (a) _____

    (b) _____

    (c) _____

(3) Name three elements of Emily Dickinson's poems that are praised today.

    (a) _____

    (b) _____

    (c) _____

STUDYING THE PASSAGE

(1) Find the Main Idea: Choose one answer.
    (a) Why Emily Dickinson became a recluse.
    (b) Why Emily Dickinson wrote poetry.
    (c) Emily Dickinson's life.
    (d) Emily Dickinson's likes and dislikes. _____

(2) Find the Facts: Mark each one *true* or *false*.
    (a) Emily lived in the city.   (a) _____
    (b) Emily had a happy childhood.   (b) _____

(c) Emily never learned to tell the time by a clock.   (c) _____

(d) Emily was happy at college.   (d) _____

(e) Some think Emily was greatly disappointed in love.   (e) _____

(f) Emily knew nothing about Shakespeare's writing.   (f) _____

(g) She kept her poems in a locked closet.   (g) _____

(h) Emily wore only black dresses after she became a recluse.   (h) _____

(3) Find the Order: Number the following in the order in which they appear in the passage.

(a) She shunned all but her closest family.   (a) _____

(b) Her poems are praised for their originality.   (b) _____

(c) Here she proved an apt, hard-working, and enthusiastic student.   (c) _____

(d) Emily developed a style unique for her time.   (d) _____

(e) She would spend happy hours sharing confidences with them.   (e) _____

(f) They lived in a large, comfortable house.   (f) _____

(g) It was discovered that she had written over 1200 poems.   (g) _____

(h) "I find ecstasy in living; the mere sense of living is joy enough."   (h) _____

(4) Go beyond the Facts: Why did Emily write poetry?

(a) For fame.

(b) For money.

(c) For publication.

(d) For her personal reasons.   _____

(5) Determine the Writer's Style and Technique: Which *one* of the following does the writer do?

(a) Presents information about Emily found only in her poems.

(b) Describes Emily's personality as well as the events in her life.

(c) Describes the kind of person Emily was by relating just one incident in detail.

(d) Tells you what other people thought of Emily.   _____

USING THE WORDS

(1) Words and Their Meanings: Find the boldfaced word which fits each of these definitions.

_____ (a) keenly intelligent and responsive

_____ (b) exact in every detail

_____ (c) a statement that seems to contradict itself or seems false, but that may be true in fact

_____ (d) filled with pain and distress

_____ (e) marked by concise, clear expression

_____ (f) state of overwhelming emotion; pure delight

_____ (g) suitable for being sung or set to music; expressing intense emotion

_____ (h) avoided deliberately and habitually

_____ (i) a soft wool fabric with a colorful, swirled pattern of curved shapes

(2) Write a paragraph using three of the words from the list above. Use a separate piece of paper.

WRITING ABOUT IT

Use a separate piece of paper.

(1) What do you think Emily Dickinson was like? Read more about her life and poetry, then describe the kind of person she was. Include how she changed in her early thirties and tell about the poems she wrote.

(2) Imagine that you are Emily Dickenson and write a poem in a style she would have used. Show the poem to your teacher.